Our Holy Guest

Our Holy Guest

The Believer's Secret to Spiritual Power

James W. Tharp

Christian Renewal Ministries Publishing
Bozeman, Montana

OUR HOLY GUEST
Published by CHRISTIAN RENEWAL MINISTRIES
P.O. Box 11406, Bozeman, MT 59719
www.crmin.org

Unless otherwise identified, Scripture quotations are taken from the Holy Bible, New International Version® (NIV). Copyright ©1973, 1978, 1984 by International Bible Society. Used by permission of Zondervan Publishing House. All rights reserved.

Scripture quotations (AMP) are taken from The Amplified Bible, Old Testament copyright © 1965, 1987 by the Zondervan Corporation and The Amplified New Testament copyright © 1958, 1987 by The Lockman Foundation. Used by permission. All rights reserved.

Scripture quotations (KJV) are taken from The King James Version, The New Chain-Reference Bible, Third Improved Edition, copyright © 1957 by Frank Charles Thompson, DD., PhD., B. B. Kirkbride Bible Co., Inc. All rights reserved.

Scripture quotations (NKJV) are taken from the Holy Bible, New King James Version, copyright © 1979, 1980, 1982 by Thomas Nelson, Inc. All rights reserved.

Scripture quotations (NRSV) contained herein are from the New Revised Standard Version Bible, copyright ©1989, by the Division of Christian Education of the National Council of the Churches of Christ in the U.S.A. Used by permission. All rights reserved.

Scripture quotations taken from THE MESSAGE, copyright ©1993, 1994, 1995, 1996, 2000, 2001, 2002. Used by permission of NavPress Publishing Group. All rights reserved.

ISBN: 978-0-9846712-2-9
ISBN 978-0-9846712-3-6 – (electronic)

Copyright © 2015 James W. Tharp
jwtharp@crmin.org

All rights reserved. This book is protected by the copyright laws of the United States of America. This book may not be copied or reprinted for commercial gain or profit. The use of quotations or occasional page copying for personal or group study is permitted and encouraged.

Cover design © 2015 Marilee Donivan, Sunrise Mountain Books

Printed in the United States of America
2015 First Edition

Contents

Acknowledgments   i

Preface   iii

1. The Spirit of Holiness 1
2. The Spirit of Prayer 5
3. The Spirit of Power 11
4. The Spirit of Freedom 15
5. The Spirit of Faith 19
6. The Spirit of Inspiration 23
7. The Wind of the Spirit 27
8. The Fire of the Spirit 33
9. The Spirit of Revival 37
10. The Spirit of Truth 41
11. The Spirit of Light 45
12. The Spirit of Thanksgiving 49
13. The Spirit of Conviction 53
14. The Spirit of Assurance 57
15. The Sins Against the Spirit 61
16. The Sin of Presuming against the Spirit 67
17. The Spirit of Intercession 71
18. The Spirit of Anointing 77
19. The Spirit of the Throne & the Altar 83
20. The Spirit of Blessing 87
21. The Spirit of Burning Hearts 93
22. The Spirit of Salvation 95
23. The Holy Spirit & Second Coming of Christ ... 103
24. The Seal of the Spirit 109
25. The Holy Spirit as "The Finger of God" 115
26. The Spirit of Life 121
27. The Spirit of Jesus 127
28. "Be Filled with the Spirit" 131
29. The Fullness of the Holy Spirit 137

About the Author 147

Acknowledgments

During my 43 years of pastoring churches, I felt it was my responsibility to train the church members to disciple new believers and to reach out to the lost with the Gospel. The discipleship of believers included a clear emphasis on the Holy Spirit. The new Christians who took seriously the truths of the Spirit's work within them grew in the grace and knowledge of our Lord and Savior Jesus Christ. So many of those who only learned *about* the Holy Spirit developed a form of godliness devoid of power; those who came to *know* the Holy Spirit as indwelling, sanctifying, empowering, and anointing grew into mature, stable, fruitful witnesses for Jesus Christ.

When I left the pastoral ministry and took up an itinerant ministry of calling Christians and churches to spiritual renewal, I realized that the majority of members in most of the churches failed to understand a meaningful relationship with the Holy Spirit. They were trying to live the Christian life on their own power. Not being kept busy full-time in traveling and preaching gave me time for writing. In 1986 the Lord led me to launch a quarterly periodical that I call the *Christian Renewal Journal*. Messages on the Holy Spirit that I had been giving to churches, camp meetings, and conferences I began publishing in the *Journal*. The feedback was much the same as in the renewal services—interest, hunger, and responses to the invitation to come and pray for a fresh filling of the Holy Spirit.

Christian Renewal Ministries operates a prayer ministry in Belgrade, Montana, that we call THE BIG SKY HOUSE OF PRAYER. One day, Vanessa McMurray, director of our House of Prayer said, "Why not write a book—maybe short devotionals—on the Holy Spirit?" I really felt the Spirit confirm her suggestion. When I shared her suggestion with my wife Shirley and my daughter Priscilla Larsen, who is my executive assistant, they both agreed emphatically. I continued praying and within a few months began writing and rewriting some of the material that reportedly the Spirit had used to draw many to a meaningful relationship with the Holy Spirit.

It is my growing conviction that unless the Church returns to Pentecostal power we shall never see the Spirit-anointed intercessors required for the kind of historic spiritual awakening so desperately needed to prepare Christians for the Second Coming of Jesus Christ. May the Holy Spirit awaken believers everywhere to the need for rekindling holy fire and for praying for the kind of revival that will lead to heart holiness, sacrificial prayer, sincere worship, and a restoration of the glory of God on His people.

I am extremely grateful to my wife Shirley for her relentless weeks of editing and her wisdom and tireless efforts to help me bring this work about.

A debt of gratitude is owed Marilee Donivan for her artistic work in designing the book cover and her completion of the book's formatting.

Preface

The concept that God is Spirit is found in many religions, but the doctrine of the personality of the Holy Spirit is a unique element of Christianity. The "Holy Ghost" in the Hebrew Scriptures is identified as the "Holy Spirit" in the Christian Scriptures. His importance can be seen by His prominence throughout the Bible—He is mentioned on the first page (Genesis 1:2), on the last page (Revelation 22:17), and hundreds of times in between.

Many still refer to the Spirit of God as the "Holy Ghost," but since the term "ghost" conjures up vague imaginations of haunting emanations and nebulous influences, I prefer the term "Spirit." Actually, as a Christian believer, I prefer to refer to the Holy Spirit as my "*Holy Guest*," because Jesus made His followers a promise: ". . . I will ask the Father, and he will give you another Counselor to be with you forever—the Spirit of truth. The world cannot accept him, because it neither sees him nor knows him. But you know him, for he lives with you and will be in you" (John 14:16-17). *With* you and *in* you, Jesus promised us—the indwelling *Guest* of the truly born-again believer! The apostle Paul sought to impress the Corinthian believers with this holy intimacy by asking, "Do you not know that your body is a temple of the Holy Spirit, who is in you, whom you have received from God? You are not your own; you were bought at a price. Therefore honor God with your body" (I Corinthians 6:19-20).

The Hebrew term for "Spirit" is *ruach*, and in the Greek it is *pneuma*. The same is used for "wind" and "breath." So the Holy Spirit is not an imaginary entity; He is the divine breath upon the spiritual life of the Christian believer. He is a member of the Triune Godhead. The Holy Spirit is God, having all the attributes of God the Father and God the Son. He is to be worshiped and obeyed as God. And since He is our *Holy Guest*, we are to be His *attentive hosts*.

*****

While Jesus Christ is the supreme and final revelation of God the Father, the Holy Spirit is the divine Agent of revelation. Therefore, it is not surprising that He is shown throughout the New Testament as the Attender of Jesus from the instant of Jesus' miraculous conception to the very moment of His glorious resurrection. A distinct feature of the Christian Scriptures is Jesus' constant relationship with the Holy Spirit throughout His entire life and ministry: Jesus was the Spirit-born Son (Matthew 1:18), the Spirit-anointed Servant (Luke 4:18-19), the Spirit-enabled Sacrifice (Hebrews 9:14), and the Spirit-resurrected Lord (Romans 1:4).

While preparing His apostles for taking His Gospel to the world, Jesus' primary subject was the Holy Spirit. On His departure, He ordered them to "stay in the city until you have been clothed with power from on high" (Luke 24:49). "But you will receive power when the Holy Spirit comes on you; and you will be my witnesses in Jerusalem, and in all Judea and Samaria, and to the ends of the earth" (Acts 1:8). Knowing they would ultimately fail without the cleansing, anointing, and wisdom of the Holy Spirit, He insisted that they must return to Jerusalem and wait for the coming of the Spirit of power. They could never live holy lives; take authority over self, the world, or Satan; or proclaim His Gospel successfully apart from the power of the Holy Spirit.

It should not come as a surprise that the Lord's chosen apostle to write most of the New Testament epistles would command believers to **"be filled with the Spirit"** (Ephesians 5:18). Paul understood that Jesus knew His apostles would completely fail in carrying out their Master's mandate of a global Gospel enterprise if they launched their mission apart from the power of the Holy Spirit (Acts 1:8).

I dare to claim that after two thousand years of church history, the believer's greatest need today is a clearer understanding of the Holy Spirit. Many of His followers know some *facts about* the Holy Spirit but so few know the *fullness of* the Spirit.

May the Holy Spirit Himself help the writer and reader to glorify our Lord Jesus Christ in thanking Him and our Heavenly Father for giving us the gift of our Holy Guest in order that we might become *holy hosts*—humble, hungry, honest seekers of the Holy Spirit. May it be said of us, even as it was of those believers on the day of Pentecost after their days of praying, "All of them were filled with the Holy Spirit" (Acts 2:4).

James W. Tharp
Bozeman, Montana

1

The Spirit of Holiness

" . . . Who is like you—majestic in holiness, awesome in glory, working wonders?" (Exodus 15:11).

Andrew Murray considered divine holiness to be "more than a divine attribute, but the comprehensive summary of all God's perfections." As my late friend Dr. William M. Greathouse used to say, "The truth of Christian holiness is so grand that it defies any finality of expression." Nevertheless, all true Christian believers feel the need to partake more deeply of and proclaim more powerfully the glories of the holiness of God the Father, God the Son, and God the Holy Spirit.

Since God is absolutely and eternally holy, He wants a holy people. Though no human can be as holy as God, He calls us to "Be holy, because I am holy" (I Peter 1:16). God's gracious plan of salvation provides for our forgiveness of sin in the new birth experience (justification by faith). But that salvation by grace extends to the justified believer in cleansing from sin (sanctification by faith).

In the new birth experience the penitent believer receives the Holy Spirit as a gift. On the day of Pentecost, Peter told the crowd who sought to know what they must do to be saved, "Repent and be baptized, every one of you, in the name of Jesus Christ for the forgiveness of your sins. And you will receive the gift of the Holy Spirit" (Acts 2:38). The apostle Paul reminded his readers of the meaning of the gift of the Spirit in their conversion experience: "And you also were included in Christ when you heard the word of truth, the gospel of your salvation. Having believed, you were marked in him with a seal, the promised Holy Spirit" (Ephesians 1:13). The apostle went on in verse 14 to explain that the believers' gift of the Spirit marked them as Christ's possession, assuring them of their eternal inheritance in Him.

So many believers today are floundering for the lack of an understanding of how to go on into a life of fullness of the Spirit. Jesus spent much time promising the disciples the Spirit's work of convicting, comforting, and counseling them in their personal lives and public ministries. He made it clear that they were not to try and carry out His order to preach the gospel until they had been "clothed with power from on high" (Luke 24:49).

"Be filled with the Spirit" (Ephesians 5:18) was Paul's message to the Ephesians. All who are blessed with the gift of the Spirit in regeneration must come to a hunger and thirst for His fullness. With the hunger must come a seeking. With the thirst will come a faith to ask. Jesus explained that if children asked loving parents for their hearts desires (in their case, food), they would not be given something poisonous or harmful; then He said, ". . . how much more will your Father in heaven give the Holy Spirit to those who ask him" (Luke 11:13).

The Father gives the fullness of the Spirit to those who *ask*. I often preach and teach on the fullness of the Spirit, and then I learn that most professing Christians have never asked to be filled. In His teaching on the Holy Spirit Jesus commanded, "Ask and it will be given to you; seek and you will find; knock and the door will be opened to you" (Luke 11:9).

God gives the fullness of the Spirit to those who *obey*. When the apostles, who had been filled with the Spirit on the day of Pentecost went about Jerusalem in great power, the Jewish high priest and his associates ordered their arrest and charged them to no longer teach and preach in Jesus' name. These enemies of Christianity who had crucified Jesus could not understand the strange powers of Christ's followers to heal the sick, walk through locked prison doors, and handle persecution with poise and dignity. Peter explained, "We are witnesses of these things, and so is the Holy Spirit, whom God has given to those who obey him" (Acts 5:32). Peter wanted every member of the Jewish

Sanhedrin to know that those who were now preaching had not only been filled with the Spirit because of their obedience to Christ's commands but they were also operating out of that fullness.

God gives the fullness of the Spirit to those who *believe*. The Lord is helping me in these times as I minister to empty, disheartened, professing Christians. They sit in their pews with friendly faces, but many are wearing masks—angry at their emptiness and skeptical about what they are hearing, but heartened by an urge to pray for a true sense of the presence and power of God in their lives.

Then as I preach the Word, I feel a fresh inspiration—the cold front is passing, the atmosphere is being flushed, and I know that the prayers of intercessors, both present and absent, are driving back the darkness of doubt and depression. Ears and hearts are being conditioned for hearing. Hunger is deepening. Choices are going to be made.

Prayer: Heavenly Father, thank You for sending Jesus Christ, Your Son, to die on the cross to atone for all my sins. And thank You for sending the Holy Spirit, the very Spirit of the Father and the Spirit of Your Son to indwell, sanctify, comfort, counsel, and empower me to live the Christian life. I know Your Holy Spirit is in me, but I now ask You to fill me with Your Spirit. *"Wash me thoroughly from my iniquity, and cleanse me from my sin . . . Create in me a clean heart, O God, and renew a steadfast spirit within me. Do not cast me away from Your presence, and do not take Your Holy Spirit from me. Restore to me the joy of Your salvation, and uphold me by Your generous Spirit"* (Psalm 51:2, 10-12, NKJV).

O God, Your Word tells me that I was predestined to become transformed into the likeness of Jesus by the workings of the Spirit within me to walk in righteousness and true holiness. And now, Father God, thank You for sanctifying me completely—spirit, soul, and body—and preserving me blameless until the coming of our Lord Jesus Christ. Amen!

2

The Spirit of Prayer

". . . the Spirit helps us in our weakness. We do not know what we ought to pray for, but the Spirit himself intercedes for us with groans that words cannot express. And he who searches our hearts knows the mind of the Spirit, because the Spirit intercedes for the saints in accordance with God's will" (Romans 8:26-27).

"And pray in the Spirit on all occasions with all kinds of prayers and requests. With this in mind, be alert and always keep on praying for all the saints" (Ephesians 6:18).

"But you, dear friends, build yourselves up in your most holy faith and pray in the Holy Spirit" (Jude 20).

The disciples must have been absolutely amazed as Jesus "full of joy through the Holy Spirit" (Luke 10:21) overflowed in praise to the Father. They were certainly impressed with His unceasing practice of prayer—Mark 1:35, 14:32-42; Luke 5:16, 11:1. After a short time with Him, they discovered that prayer was not merely a seasoning for their Master's life; *prayer was His life!* They realized He was not just saying prayers; He was getting answers. Finally, they were driven to ask their

Lord the secret of His power in prayer.

They received their answer in Luke 11:1-4; Jesus not only gave a model prayer, He continued with a parable on prayer, sometimes referred to as "The Midnight Mediator" (vv. 5-8). Finally, after insisting that true intercessory prayer includes the stages of asking, seeking, and knocking (vv. 9-10), he gives them the secret in vv. 11-13: "Which of you fathers, if your son asks for a fish, will give him a snake instead? Or if he asks for an egg, will give him a scorpion? If you then, though you are evil, know how to give good gifts to your children, how much more will your Father in heaven give the Holy Spirit to those who ask him!" Jesus gave His twelve disciples a model prayer that contains all the aspects of true communion with God—*adoration, confession, petition,* and *intercession.*

When we believers begin our daily season of prayer with *adoration,* the Spirit responds within us with conviction, sensitivity, and inspiration. We sense our failures, sins, and strongholds where Satan has taken advantage of us and where we slipped into selfish thoughts, words, and actions.

Then we go into *confession*; "If we confess our sins, he is faithful and just and will forgive us our sins and purify us from all unrighteousness" (I John 1:9). With the freshness of forgiveness and the freedom of purity, we are now ready to obey our Lord and ask for the "much-moreness" (abundance, fullness) of the Holy Spirit, believing that our Father in heaven gladly awaits to "give the Holy Spirit to those who ask him" (Luke 11:13). As believers, we already have the indwelling of the Holy Spirit, but we are commanded by our Lord to call in prayer for His sanctifying fullness. Only then are we enlightened to continue our *petitions* and then empowered to move into *intercession.*

Intercession is priestly praying—appealing on behalf of earthly needs before our heavenly Father—praying for saints to be holy, sinners to be saved, communities to live in righteousness, nations to glorify God, and for the church throughout the world to be revived. Another Bible term for *intercession* is *supplication,* meaning "to plead for earnestly." The Holy Spirit in cleansing and empowering the believer for prayer is masterful in inspiring us for *supplication*—"Pray in the Spirit at all times in every prayer and supplication. To that end keep alert and always persevere in supplication for all the saints" (Ephesians 6:18, NRSV).

The greatest hindrance to prayer in the church today is our ignorance of what Jesus taught concerning the role of the Holy Spirit in the believer's prayer life. The tragic lack of understanding cost this writer thirty years of mediocrity in pastoral ministry. Before we can obey the call to "pray in the Spirit" we must first be "born of the Spirit" (John 3:3-8), "sanctified by the Spirit" (Romans 15:16), and "filled with the Spirit" (Ephesians 5:18).

What does it mean to pray in the Spirit? We need the humility to confess with the apostle Paul that, left to our natural abilities, we are weak when it comes to prayer. He wrote, ". . . the Spirit helps us in our weakness. We do not know what we ought to pray for . . ." (Romans 8:26). I wish to share three ways in which the Holy Spirit helps our praying:

1. *The Holy Spirit enlightens our understanding so that we pray according to the will of God.* Our hope for success in prayer begins at the point of our humility to acknowledge our lack of understanding this marvelous spiritual grace of prayer. The Holy Spirit understands it perfectly because He is God and knows the requests the Father wants us to express, because they are the ones He wants to answer. The sanctified heart yields to the will of God, just as Jesus did when he prayed, and "the Spirit intercedes for the saints in accordance with God's will" (Romans 8:27). Only as we follow the discerned directions for prayer can we be certain of YES answers. But, how rewarding to pray the will of God to pass in our lives, in our families, and in our churches!

2. *The Holy Spirit energizes our human spirit so that we do not faint.* Jesus and His apostles were faithful to warn against fainting at the sacred call to prayer. On Mount Hermon and in the Garden of Gethsemane, Peter, James, and John fainted at their assigned posts of prayer. ". . . Jesus told his disciples a parable to show them that they should always pray and not give up" (Luke 18:1). Even Jesus relied on the energy and inspiration of the Holy Spirit. Unless we do the same, we'll discover a lack of interest in prayer, an absence of inspiration, and a wavering in our discipline. Samuel Chadwick would often charge Christian leaders with the piercing words, "Brethren, the crying sin of the church is her laziness after God." Isaiah seemed to be deploring this kind of apathy when he observed, "No one calls on your name or

strives to lay hold of you" (Isaiah 64:7). My prayer partner Dr. Wesley Duewel says in his book, *Mighty Prevailing Prayer,* Zondervan Publishing House, p. 55:

> Some people have to prevail over personal laziness or restlessness. They are too undisciplined to find prolonged praying possible. They need to determine by the grace of God to learn to discipline themselves. They can make this need a special object of prayer and receive God's help.

3. *The Holy Spirit enables our boldness of faith so that we will not be denied.* I've often presented prayer as *worship, work,* and *warfare.* In presenting prayer as warfare, Paul wrote, "Finally, be strong in the Lord and in His mighty power. Put on the whole armor of God so that you can take your stand against the devil's schemes. For our struggle is not against flesh and blood, but against the rulers, against the authorities, against the powers of this dark world and against the spiritual forces of evil in the heavenly realms. Therefore put on the whole armor of God, so that when the day of evil comes, you may be able to stand your ground . . ." (Ephesians 6:10-13).

If we are truly filled, cleansed, and empowered by the Holy Spirit, we are vested with the authority of our Risen, Enthroned Christ. As His ambassadors, witnesses, and representatives on earth, we are commanded to boldly wage war against the invisible forces of evil. Too many Christians are intimidated by the world, are mired in fleshly desires, and have forgotten their untapped source of power.

By a bold faith Moses witnessed the Red Sea part for God's people to be delivered and then saw their enemies destroyed by the same miracle.

By a bold faith David faced Goliath, declaring, "You come against me with sword and spear and javelin, but I come against you in the name of the Lord Almighty, the God of the armies of Israel, whom you have defied. This day the Lord will hand you over to me, and I'll strike you down and cut off your head. Today I will give the carcasses of the Philistine army to the birds of the air and the beasts of the earth, and the whole world will know that there is a God in Israel. All those gathered here will know that it is not by sword or spear that the Lord saves, for the battle is the Lord's, and he will give all of you into our hands" (I Samuel 17:45-47).

Isn't it time for emboldened American believers to answer God's call back to the Upper Room for a fresh filling of the Holy Spirit? Then, empowered by the Holy Spirit, we can go out to speak the promise of revival to a paralyzed church, to preach the Gospel of hope to lost souls, and to offer a divine intervention to an imploding nation.

Prayer: O God, forgive my sin of prayerlessness. It is Your command that I "pray without ceasing." But I must confess that I have failed to schedule my prayer time and have allowed other things to crowd it out. I confess that at times I've even lost an interest in prayer. I've grown careless and empty.

Please, Lord, fill me with the Holy Spirit until I'm enlightened and energized for prayer and emboldened in prayer. I long to become so caught up in communion with You that I lose the sense of time and realize there is nothing better than holy fellowship with the Holy Trinity. Amen!

3

The Spirit of Power

"I am going to send you what my Father has promised; but stay in the city until you have been clothed with power from on high" (Luke 24:49).

"But you will receive power when the Holy Spirit comes on you; and you will be my witnesses in Jerusalem, and in all Judea and Samaria, and to the ends of the earth" (Acts 1:8).

"May the God of hope fill you with all joy and peace as you trust in him, so that you may overflow with hope by the power of the Holy Spirit" (Romans 15:13).

The greatest tragedy within Christendom is that many believers ignore the amazing, infinite power available to them through the indwelling Holy Spirit. Twice in his epistles the apostle John wrote: ". . . God is love" (I John 4:8, 16). In fact, in studying John's first epistle we learn that love is not merely an attribute of God; it is the absolute essence of His divine Being. While there are other divine attributes, love is the defining one. This means that our Heavenly Father, our Lord Jesus Christ, and our indwelling Holy Spirit share this amazing attribute of love! The Holy Trinity—God the Father, God the Son, and God the Holy Spirit—demonstrated this amazing love on Calvary's cross when

Jesus Christ shed His blood for our redemption.

The Holy Spirit is the Spirit of love. He comes into the believer's heart in the new birth (Acts 2:38; Ephesians 1:13), and the apostle Paul tells us, "God has poured out his love into our hearts by the Holy Spirit, whom he has given us" (Romans 5:5).

God never intended that Christians live the Christian life on their own strength. Divine love is the greatest force in the universe. This force or power is manifested in several ways:

• *Power to believe in Jesus Christ as Savior*. The apostle Paul also tells us that "no one can say, 'Jesus is Lord,' except by the Holy Spirit" (I Corinthians 12:3). A friend or loved one may appeal to someone to become a believer, and a preacher of the Gospel may appeal for a penitent person to come forward and confess Jesus Christ. But no human being can convict unbelievers of their sin, their lostness, their need of a Savior. This serious act must be performed by the Holy Spirit. Jesus promised that the Spirit would "convict the world of sin, and of righteousness, and of judgment: of sin, because they do not believe in Me" (John 16:8-9, NKJV).

• *Power to love God with all our hearts and power to love others and forgive them*. When believers experience the new birth, there is a transformation—we are given a new nature. In theological terms it is called "regeneration." It means rebirth, a new creation, a new disposition. When the Holy Spirit administers God's grace of regeneration He begins to release God's love into our hearts enabling us to forgive ourselves and our enemies. Such power is not automatically generated, but as we pray for grace, God's love is released into us and we grow in our love for God. The more we love God, the easier it becomes to forgive. Jesus warned, "But if you do not forgive men their sins, your Father will not forgive your sins" (Matthew 6:15). Only by drawing prayerfully on the power of the Spirit within us are we able to forgive and love as we are commanded.

• *Power to resist temptation and live a holy life*. The apostle Paul made it clear to Christians that we are not exempt from temptation. In Romans 8:2-14, he mentions two inner opposing forces—"the mind-set of the flesh" and "the mind-set of the Spirit"—with which we must deal responsibly. To yield to the fleshly mind-set leads to spiritual death. Therefore, the apostle reminds believers that *if the Spirit of God lives in them,* they "are controlled not by the sinful nature but by the Spirit" (v. 9). Paul is telling us that we are not powerless when it comes to the appeal for selfish living. We are to remember the enabling power of the Spirit to help us rise up and say no to the enemy. "For if you live according to [the dictates of] the flesh you will surely die. But if through the power of the (Holy) Spirit you are habitually putting to death—make extinct, deaden—the [evil] deeds prompted by the body, you shall (really and genuinely) live forever" (Romans 8:13, AMP). Our power to live the holy life is not of ourselves; it is available to us through the indwelling Holy Spirit who awaits our call for strength against anything that threatens our fellowship with God.

• *Power to pray.* We cannot even have a meaningful prayer life apart from the power of the Holy Spirit. Listen to Paul's explanation: ". . . the Spirit helps us in our weakness. We do not know what we ought to pray for, but the Spirit himself intercedes for us with groans that words cannot express. And he who searches our hearts knows the mind of the Spirit, because the Spirit intercedes for the saints in accordance with God's will" (Romans 8:26-27). The Holy Spirit will impress us to pray according to the will of God. When we are sensitive to Him, He will bring us into agreement with the way our Savior is praying, and we will see answers to prayer.

• *Power to witness.* Just before His ascension to the Father, Jesus promised, "But you will receive power when the Holy Spirit comes on you; and you will be my witnesses . . ." (Acts 1:8). This command and promise was given to the apostles as well as other believers, so it applies to every believer. Unfortunately, not all believers are filled with the Spirit. Many have grown cold, worldly, and uncaring. But Spirit-filled believers are aware of Christ's commission to reach out to the lost and share the good news of God's love for everyone. We are to call on the Spirit to help us witness to the unsaved. We need to be alert to the Spirit's leadership as to whom we are to witness, and how and when. In His wisdom we go to the lost in love, with respect, and filled with joy and enthusiasm over what Christ has done for us and what He wants to do for those we want to see become followers of our Lord.

* *Power to serve*. All believers are under orders to do works of righteousness. We are not saved by works, but we show our appreciation to God for saving us by doing good works. "For it is by grace you have been saved, through faith—and this not from yourselves, it is the gift of God—not by works, so that no one can boast. For we are God's workmanship, created in Christ Jesus to do good works, which God prepared in advance for us to do" (Ephesians 2:8-10).

Every believer has been given spiritual gifts, and we should each work for the Lord according to the Spirit's gifting and as the Spirit leads us. We can all pray, give, witness, encourage, and worship.

Let it be remembered that even though we are saved by grace, we shall be judged by our works in that day when we give an account of our stewardship to the Lord. "For we must all appear before the judgment seat of Christ, that each one may receive what is due him for the things done while in the body, whether good or bad" (II Corinthians 5:10). By our good works we are laying up treasures in heaven. Our labors of love, our sacrifices made for advancing the kingdom of God, our efforts to reach the lost with the Gospel of Jesus Christ—all these things are recorded, and we will be rewarded according to our faithfulness.

Prayer: Lord, forgive our powerlessness! We're ashamed of our deadness, apathy, carelessness, and unconcern about spiritual matters. For too long we have ignored Your call to a life of power. Breathe on us, Holy Spirit. Burn the chaff from our heart and life to prepare us for service to You. We do want to lay up treasures in Heaven and not live for this life only. We do want to love You with all our heart and our total being. We do want Your Spirit's help to deny self and live holy lives. We do want to have a meaningful prayer life.

Lord, we need Your Spirit's help to lovingly witness to our lost loved ones and friends. O God, we must not waste the years of our life. So empower us to work for You. "And whatever you (we) do, whether in word or deed, (may we) do it all in the name of the Lord Jesus, giving thanks to the Father through Him" (Colossians 3:17). Amen!

4

The Spirit of Freedom

"... If you abide in My word, you are My disciples indeed. And you shall know the truth, and the truth shall make you free" (John 8:31-32, NKJV).

"Stand fast therefore in the liberty by which Christ has made us free, and do not be entangled again with a yoke of bondage" (Galatians 5:1, NKJV).

"Now the Lord is the Spirit, and where the Spirit of the Lord is, there is liberty—emancipation from bondage, freedom. And all of us, as with unveiled face, [because we] continued to behold [in the Word of God] as in a mirror the glory of the Lord, are constantly being transfigured into His very own image in ever increasing splendor and from one degree of glory to another; [for this comes] from the Lord [Who is] the Spirit" (II Corinthians 3:17-18, AMP).

The Holy Spirit within the believer is present to bring about the freedom that our Savior purchased for us when He died on the cross to pay the price of our redemption.

    On a hot July night in 1946 in an old two-room schoolhouse in southeastern Arkansas, I heard a Gospel message assuring me that God loved me so much that He sacrificed His only Son, Jesus Christ, to suffer a traumatic death in payment for my sins. The evangelist stated that if I would confess my sins and come and call upon Jesus' name for salvation and place my faith in Him as my Lord and Savior, I would be forgiven and have peace with God. He also said that the Holy Spirit, the Spirit of God the Father and God the Son, would come to live in my heart. What a powerful message! I'd heard it in part before, but I had never been as impressed as I was at that moment. I went forward, knelt at an altar, confessed my sins, asked God for the gift of eternal life, and believed in Jesus Christ as my Savior!

My first sense of reward was a *freedom from condemnation*. As I arose from the altar, I noticed my Aunt BettyLee seated near the end of the aisle I would pass on my way back to where I'd been sitting. I stopped and sat with her. She congratulated me and asked, "How do you feel?" I answered with joy, "Aunt BettyLee, I feel at peace with God! That old feeling of condemnation is gone! I'm forgiven! I'm free! I'm a new person!" She hugged me and said, "I'm glad for you, son! Just stay close to Jesus and follow Him!"

Later on, under the guidance of my dear mother, Estelle, I asked, "What all really happened to me the other night when I was born-again?" She answered, "Son, read John, chapter three, and you'll understand the answer to your question better than I can explain it, because Jesus is explaining the new birth to Nicodemus, a great theologian. Yet, he had come to Jesus for some answers to his own spiritual problems."

I read John 3:16 with the joy of recalling my mother having quoted it, as well as the evangelist a few nights before when I surrendered my heart to Christ: "For God so loved the world, that he gave his only begotten Son, that whosoever believeth in him should not perish but have everlasting life" (KJV). But it was the next few verses that touched me so powerfully: "For God sent not his Son into the world to condemn the world; but that the world through him might be saved. He that believeth on him is not condemned: but he that believeth not is condemned already, because he hath not believed in the name of the only begotten Son of God. And this is the condemnation, that light is come into the world, and men loved darkness rather than light, because their deeds were evil" (John 3:17-19, KJV). I was forgiven, free from condemnation!

Another freedom came with it: *free from the fear of death*. I had feared dying because I realized I would go to hell. Now that I was saved, I no longer feared death. Oh, I loved life, especially now—I could worship God, commune with Him in prayer, fellowship with His people, and witness to my unsaved friends and encourage them to give their hearts to Christ. But almost daily I thanked God that in giving my heart to Christ I no longer dreaded death.

I was now *free to pursue God's purpose for my life.* Before trusting Christ as my Savior, I had been caught up in having a good time, running with a crowd of pleasure seekers. Now that was behind me, and I could think and pray about my reason for being on earth. What would the Lord have me be and do? Again, my Christian parents were helpful as they counseled me, "Go ahead and finish high school, and perhaps even before you graduate you'll have a good sense of what the Lord wants you to do."

Maintaining our spiritual freedom comes through sensitivity to the Holy Spirit—responding to His constraints and restraints. We learn how easy it is to lose our freedom when we are too slow to yield to His leadings and bend to His whispers. But we also learn how gracious our God is to forgive us for our failures to obey Him. The apostle John writes to believers with instructions for getting back on track with God when we fail Him: "If we confess our sins, he is faithful and just and will forgive us our sins and purify us from all unrighteousness" (I John 1:9).

Prayer: Heavenly Father, I thank You for the forgiveness of sin through our Lord Jesus Christ, who suffered a cruel death on Calvary's cross to set me free from condemnation and from the fear of death and hell. And thank You for setting me free from the fear of a wasted life. You saved me for a purpose. May I learn to stay on course with You in obedience to Your Word, Your Spirit, and Your will. I am grateful for Your Spirit's conviction when I fall short and when I am slow to obey.

Lord, I confess that I am not all that You want me to be. Please give me a passion to know You better and experience the freedom I need for worshiping You, for praying, and for witnessing to others. Amen!

5

The Spirit of Faith

"Therefore I tell you that no one who is speaking by the Spirit of God says, 'Jesus be cursed,' and no one can say, 'Jesus is Lord,' except by the Holy Spirit" (I Corinthians 12:3).

The Christian life is a life of faith. The Gospel of Jesus Christ is a gospel of faith. Paul the apostle testified, "I am not ashamed of the gospel, because it is the power of God for the salvation of everyone who believes: . . ." (Romans 1:16). And he continues: "For in the gospel a righteousness from God is revealed, a righteousness that is by faith from first to last, just as it is written: 'The righteous will live by faith'" (Romans 1:17).

• *Saving faith.* First, there is *saving faith*. This comes from the Holy Spirit, who before our new birth is not yet abiding within us. He is the divine force let loose on the world to call lost souls to God through a new spiritual birth, without which Jesus declared no one can see the kingdom of God (John 3:3). The Holy Spirit works a marvelous condition in the heart and mind of the sinner before he can repent of sin and believe in and confess Jesus Christ as Savior and Lord. As the apostle Paul stated in the above Scripture, "no one can say that 'Jesus is Lord,' except by the Holy Spirit." It is an essential mental-spiritual condition which Jesus called *conviction* (John 16:8). No one is truly ready to repent of sin and trust in Jesus Christ alone as Savior until the Holy Spirit is allowed to convince that person of his or her lostness, sinfulness, and need of Jesus Christ, the only Savior. With the proper response of honesty and humility comes the gift of *faith*. "For it is by grace you have been saved, through faith—and this not from yourselves, it is the gift of God—not by works, so that no one can boast. For we are God's workmanship, created in Christ Jesus to do good works, which God prepared in advance for us to do" (Ephesians 2:8-10).

• *Sanctifying faith.* Second, in every true believer's life there must come *sanctifying faith*. "It is God's will that you should be sanctified . . ." (I Thessalonians 4:3). Sanctification is a Bible term that any believer should study and experience. Christian theologians have come to accept it in its two-fold meaning: (1) *Cleansing* from sin, or *heart purity*; and (2) *Consecration,* yielding oneself to God for His purpose.

Sanctification is begun in regeneration, for the Holy Spirit is given to us when we are saved (Acts 2:38, Ephesians 1:13-14). Early in one's Christian life there should come a discovery of two opposing mind-sets striving for dominance—the mind-set of the flesh and the mind-set of the Spirit (Romans 8:1-17). In this passage the apostle is calling for both a cleansing and a consecration, but the *cleansing* must be an act of divine grace, for Paul writes in verse 13: ". . . if through the power of the (Holy) Spirit you are habitually putting to death—make extinct, deaden—the [evil] deeds prompted by the body, you shall (really and genuinely) live forever" (AMP). *Consecration* must be a yielding of our total self to Jesus Christ.

Sanctification is both a crisis experience and a progressive process. A. W. Tozer dramatically describes the believer who is convicted of his carnal failures and is prayerfully prepared to seek the cleansing from sin which God has promised. He writes: "When we have dealt with our carnal ambitions; when we have trodden upon the lion and adder of the flesh, have trampled the dragon of self-love under our feet and have truly reckoned ourselves to have died unto sin, then and only then can God raise us to newness of life and fill us with His blessed Holy Spirit." (A. W. Tozer, *Tozer on the Holy Spirit: A 366-Day Devotional,* Wingspread Publishers, 2000, January 17).

The initial moment of sanctification sets the stage for the fullness of the Spirit. Unfortunately, many believers only seek the cleansing, but they should, on the same occasion, ask to be filled with the Spirit. Jesus promised, "If you then, though you are evil, know how to give good gifts to your children, how much more will your Father in heaven give the Holy Spirit to those who ask him" (Luke 11:13).

Even after our crisis experience of sanctification we learn that life in the Spirit brings fresh convictions of falling short of God's glory, and we are convicted by the Spirit to repent. We read in Hebrews 2:11 about "those who are being sanctified" (NKJV). Life in the Spirit will include times when the believer will be convicted of falling short of God's will. At such times in my own life I have shamefully confessed my selfishness, slowness to obey, lack of inspiration for prayer, or distraction from the Word. As the Spirit convicts, I acknowledge my sins, confess them, and accept God's forgiveness, according to I John 1:9. With the psalmist I pray, "Create in me a clean heart, O God, and renew a steadfast spirit within me. Do not cast me away from Your presence, and do not take Your Holy Spirit from me. Restore to me the joy of Your salvation, and uphold me *by Your* generous Spirit" (Psalm 51:10-12, NKJV). Most of us need times of renewal in order to live the sanctified life and bear the fruit of the Spirit.

• *Serving faith.* Third, there is *serving faith.* We are called to be stewards of God's kingdom. There are commands to be obeyed, burdens to be born, and responsibilities to be assumed. The apostle Paul told the Corinthian believers that "it is required in stewards that one be found faithful" (I Corinthians 4:2, NKJV). We soon learn how desperately we need the help of the Holy Spirit in complying with the Scriptures and obeying the leadings of the Spirit. For at the end of life we know we shall give an account of our stewardship. "For we must all appear before the judgment seat of Christ, that each one may receive the things *done* in the body, according to what he has done, whether good or bad" (II Corinthians 5:10, NKJV).

Prayer: Lord, we are thankful for Your faithfulness in helping us follow You. We thank You for sending the Holy Spirit to be our Helper.

Without His help we will fail in the things You've called us to be and do and say. Keep reminding us that apart from You we can do nothing, and that it is only as we abide in You that we can bear fruit. When we falter, may we not give up, but ask for Your forgiveness and seek a fresh filling of the Holy Spirit. Amen!

6

The Spirit of Inspiration

"The Lord God formed the man from the dust of the ground and breathed into his nostrils the breath of life, and the man became a living being" (Genesis 2:7).

". . . he breathed on them and said, 'Receive the Holy Spirit'" (John 20:22).

"When the day of Pentecost came, they were all together in one place. Suddenly a sound like the blowing of a violent wind came from heaven and filled the whole house where they were sitting" (Acts 2:1-2).

"Then he said to me, 'Prophesy to the breath; prophesy, son of man, and say to it, 'This is what the Sovereign Lord says: Come from the four winds, O breath, and breathe into these slain, that they may live.' So I prophesied as he commanded me, and breath entered them; they came to life and stood up on their feet—a vast army" (Ezekiel 37:9-10).

The born-again experience is a miracle of spiritual resurrection. The Holy Spirit convinces a sinner of his or her lostness and brings about an inner repentance and faith, resurrecting the penitent believer from death to life. The Spirit breathes life into the believing soul, and "he is a new creation; the old has gone, the new has come" (II Corinthians 5:17).

A sound like the blowing of a violent wind that came from heaven filling the Upper Room on the day of Pentecost represented the life-giving breath of the Holy Spirit. The 120 praying believers were "all filled with the Holy Spirit" (Acts 2:4, NKJV). The church was not stillborn, but vitally, radiantly alive.

The Risen Christ made a surprise visit to His followers only a few hours after His resurrection. "He breathed on *them,* and said to them, 'Receive the Holy Spirit' . . ." (John 20:22, NKJV). He uttered a promise, a prophecy to be fulfilled in a few weeks at Pentecost. Their ten days of praying would give them time to *exhale*—empty out the toxic elements of their greed, pride, and self-centeredness; prepare them to *inhale* the breathing of the Holy Spirit upon them; and prepare them for receiving the cleansing and filling of the Holy Spirit.

It was an inspired group of Spirit-filled believers that filed out of the Upper Room and down to street level and began powerfully declaring the praises of God and preaching the Gospel of Jesus Christ to the multitude of pilgrims filling Jerusalem. Peter and John were so inspired as they approached the temple for prayer that a man crippled from birth was attracted to them. He begged money from them, but Peter said, "Silver or gold I do not have, but what I have I give you. In the name of Jesus Christ of Nazareth, walk. . . . He jumped to his feet and began to walk" (Acts 3:3-8). When Peter and John were imprisoned by the Sanhedrin and ordered to no longer speak or teach in the name of Jesus, Peter replied, "Rulers and elders of the people! . . . It is by the name of Jesus Christ of Nazareth, whom you crucified but whom God raised from the dead, that this man stands before you healed. He is the stone you builders rejected, which has become the capstone. Salvation is found in no one else, for there is no other name under heaven given to men by which we must be saved" (Acts 4:8-12).

By the inspiration of the Holy Spirit, the Gospel was preached in Jerusalem, Judea, and Samaria and has continued to be proclaimed throughout the world for more than two thousand years. Let each of us in these days pray for fresh fillings of the Spirit from time to time so that we can go forth with the same inspiration for *prayer*, *searching the Scriptures*, and *witnessing* as did the early church.

- *Inspiration for prayer.* The Holy Spirit specializes in enabling the believer for prayer. According to the apostle Paul, the Spirit offsets our ignorance and weaknesses with inspiration as He "intercedes for us with groans that words cannot express" and this always "in accordance with God's will" (Romans 8:26-27). The apostle James wrote, "The effective, fervent prayer of a righteous man avails much" (James 5:16, NKJV). God loves a prayer that is prayed with fervency, feeling, emotion, and inspiration. Whether prayed in shouts of joy or tears of grief, God pays attention to the sincerity, passion, and feeling behind the prayer. We need not try to work up our emotions; we simply allow the Holy Spirit within us to inspire our faith and feelings as we make our case before the Throne of Grace.

- *Inspiration for searching the Scriptures.* "All Scripture is God-breathed and is useful for teaching, rebuking, correcting and training in righteousness, so that the man of God may be thoroughly equipped for every good work" (II Timothy 3:16-17). The same Holy Spirit who breathed on the writer of Scripture also wants to breathe on the reader of Scripture for understanding. And whether we are being taught, rebuked, corrected, or trained, the inspiration will hold if we decide to receive His Word for living in obedience to our Lord.

- *Inspiration for witnessing.* Just before His ascension back to the Father, Jesus said to His followers, ". . . you will receive power when the Holy Spirit comes on you; and you will be my witnesses in Jerusalem, and in all Judea and Samaria, and to the ends of the earth" (Acts 1:8). The Holy Spirit empowers believers with love and respect for the lost. A Spirit-filled Christian will witness with the inspiration of hope as he shares what Christ means to him and what He can bring to the person to whom he is speaking. The listener will be able to sense the life, radiance, and peace in the witness. Witnessing is more than salesmanship; it is allowing the Spirit to reveal to the hearer the joy of forgiveness and an exciting relationship with Jesus Christ, as well as the power to come to grips with the problems and pressures of life. Spirit-filled witnesses know that telling others about the love of God in offering His Son Jesus as their Savior is nothing short of "joy inexpressible and full of glory" (I Peter 1:8, NKJV).

<u>Prayer</u>: O God, forgive our prayerlessness! And forgive our lack of spirit when we try to pray. Help us remember that the Spirit within us wants to pray through us, and our Great High Priest, our Lord Jesus Christ, awaits at the right hand of the Father to hear our praises, our heart-searching cries for forgiveness, our petitions for daily needs, and our intercession for lost loved ones and friends and a needy world.

Lord, forgive us for trying to pray without the inspiration of our indwelling Holy Spirit, who wishes to initiate the prayer Himself and align our will with His will and our thoughts with His thoughts, so that we even call on Him to strengthen our faith in knowing the prayer will be answered.

Lord, teach us to pray—when, what, where, and with whom! Help us pray Your promises, claim Your Word, and pray it to pass in our personal lives, in our families, in our churches, in our nation, and in our world!

Thank You, Lord Jesus, for all You taught about prayer and that You look forward to hearing our prayers. Help us realize what we are missing by our negligence. The apostle was right—we "do not have, because (we) do not ask God," or we "do not receive because (we) ask with wrong motives" (James 4:2-3).

Teach us how to come confidently and regularly before the Throne of Grace, remembering that we have a sympathetic Intercessor who knows our every weakness, need, inability, and vulnerability. Still, we are invited to come and ask "with confidence, so that we may receive mercy and find grace to help us in our time of need" (Hebrews 4:16). Amen!

7

The Wind of the Spirit

"The wind blows wherever it pleases. You hear its sound, but you cannot tell where it comes from or where it is going . . ." (John 3:8).

"When the day of Pentecost came, they were all together in one place. Suddenly a sound like the blowing of a violent wind came from heaven and filled the whole house where they were sitting" (Acts 2:1-2).

The distinguished Jewish theologian Nicodemus could no longer deny the miraculous power of God at work in the life and ministry of the Galilean. Nor could he quench his thirst to meet Jesus face-to-face. So, humbling himself and putting his reputation on the line, he went one night to confess that Jesus was from God and inquire of him the way of salvation.

Jesus responded to Israel's prominent religious leader by making an issue of the supernatural work of the Holy Spirit. No one can enter the kingdom of God without a spiritual transformation, Jesus explained, and this requires the Spirit of God to bring about the miracle of regeneration. Just as a natural birth is necessary for one to enter and become aware of the human family, we "must be born again . . . born of the Spirit" (John 3: 5-8) in order to grasp the reality of our heavenly Father and our relationships with His kingdom. Furthermore, admission to the kingdom of God is never by the proud prerogative of race, status, nation, class, or gender. It is certainly not by heredity! All who enter the kingdom of God must be born into it by the Spirit. This spiritual birth is an act of God.

Jesus was faithful to explain to Nicodemus the one simple condition for being born again: *believing in God's one and only Son who was* "lifted up" *(crucified) for our sins* (John 3:14-21). The evidence that one has truly believed ("come into the light"), Jesus said, is that he "lives by the truth" (John 3:21).

To condition Nicodemus for accepting the sovereignty of the Holy Spirit, Jesus said, "The wind blows wherever it pleases. You hear its sound, but you cannot tell where it comes from or where it is going. So it is with everyone born of the Spirit" (John 3:8). This seeking Pharisee represented an institutional religion that thrived on writing dogmas and building walls—dogmas of condemnation and walls of exclusion. He belonged to a tradition that arrogantly drew lines and decreed, "Here, within this perimeter the grace and power of God must operate according to our set of rules, and beyond this all else is heresy and damnation!"

It seems to be the everlasting temptation of organized religion to try and direct the operations of the Holy Spirit—to say what miracles He can and cannot do and what gifts He can and cannot give, as well as to determine on whom He can and cannot fall. No, dear friends, "the wind blows wherever it pleases"—not where our pride and prejudices prohibit, not where our dogmas demand, and not where our fears forbid!

Those of us who are engaged in revival work should lead the way in repenting of our sins of spiritual pride and unbelief as shown in our attempts to control the workings and manifestations of the Holy Spirit. Sometimes we have wished for only His gentle breezes to refresh the saints, reunite the members, replenish the treasury, and restore the church's reputation in the community.

But the Spirit of revival is not always the accommodating, comforting force we had hoped for. We must be willing to let Him come as He chooses—perhaps as a tornado to destroy our idols and blow down our walls. Like Nicodemus, we need to be reminded that the Holy Spirit must be free to embarrass our rigid theological positions or bypass our ecclesiastical forms.

Dear readers, let us join with Christ's apostles and revivalists across the centuries who have surrendered their prejudices, pride, fear, dogmas, and unbelief to the sovereignty of the Holy Spirit. Then let us fast and pray and believe for the howling winds and refining fires of Pentecost. Let us allow His holy fire to burn up our chaff of unbelief, disobedience, selfishness, worldliness, and division. Then let us hoist our sails into His holy winds and prove the Spirit's power to save, sanctify, and empower us to reach our imploding nation before it is too late.

    The early church heard a sound from heaven "like the blowing of a violent wind" (Acts 2:2). This is a reminder that the church was not stillborn, but charged with eternal life. The 120 believers understood this wind to be the Holy Spirit, the very breath of God. They were moved by it. Soon they were energized to go down to the crowds filling Jerusalem with a message of eternal life. Multitudes whose religion centered around the Law were soon hearing the praises of God and the Gospel of Jesus Christ as preached by the Spirit-filled apostle Peter. And to their amazement, they heard in their own native tongues. The 120 were miraculously inspired of the Holy Spirit to utter the good news of Christ's resurrection in all of the languages represented from the Mediterranean world. They heard the apostle say, "Men of Israel, listen to this: Jesus of Nazareth was a man accredited by God to you by miracles, wonders and signs, which God did among you through him, as you yourselves know. This man was handed over to you by God's set purpose and foreknowledge; and you, with the help of wicked men, put him to death by nailing him to the cross. But God raised him from the dead, freeing him from the agony of death, because it was impossible for death to keep its hold on him" (Acts 2:22-24).

    Then Peter went on with the message of the gospel: "Therefore let all Israel be assured of this: God has made this Jesus, whom you crucified, both Lord and Christ. When the people heard this they were cut to the heart and said to Peter and the other apostles, 'Brothers, what shall we do?' Peter replied, 'Repent and be baptized, every one of you in the name of Jesus Christ for the forgiveness of your sins. And you will receive the gift of the Holy Spirit. The promise is for you and your children and for all who are far off—for all whom the Lord our God will call'" (Acts 2:36-39).

    The winds of the Spirit were blowing in Jerusalem on that first day of the Feast of Pentecost, as Peter continued to speak: "With many other words he warned them; and he pleaded with them, 'Save yourselves from this corrupt generation'" (Acts 2:40). Luke the historian reported: "Those who accepted his message were baptized, and about three thousand were added to their number that day" (Acts 2:41).

And the winds of the Spirit continued to blow, for Luke's report gets even better: "They devoted themselves to the apostles' teaching and to the fellowship, to the breaking of bread and to prayer. Everyone was filled with awe, and many wonders and miraculous signs were done by the apostles. All the believers were together and they had everything in common. Selling their possessions and goods, they gave to anyone as he had need. Every day they continued to meet together in the temple courts. They broke bread in their homes and ate together with glad and sincere hearts, praising God and enjoying the favor of all the people. And the Lord added to their number daily those who were being saved" (Acts 2:42-47).

The Holy Spirit filled, quickened, and anointed the 120 believers and continued to move mightily on the unbelieving crowds. When they were convicted of the sin of unbelief concerning what they had done to Jesus, many repented and were transformed.

Dear believers, let us pray for a fresh quickening of the Spirit today and obey Christ's commission to tell lost souls about us the good news that God wants to give them eternal life and the power of the Holy Spirit to help them live according to His will.

The anointed Scottish preacher James W. Stewart cautioned the church against quenching the Spirit:

> Don't try to tame that intractable wind. No set of Convocation or Assembly can circumscribe it, no arrogant dictator can curb it, no rooted personal prejudice can patronize it. It is master of the world. And—don't you see?—this is the essential optimism of Christianity. Here in the Spirit of Christ is a force capable of bursting into the hardest paganism, discomfiting the most rigid dogmatism, electrifying the most suffocating ecclesiasticism. This is the sovereign freedom of the Holy Spirit. There is no citadel of self and sin that is safe from Him, no unbelieving cynic secure from His reach. There is no ironclad bastion of theological self-confidence He cannot disturb into faith,

no ancient animosities He cannot reconcile. And blessed be His name, there is no winter death of the soul that He cannot quicken into a blossoming springtime, no dry bones He cannot vitalize into a marching army! This is the glory of Pentecost. (James W. Stewart, *The Wind of the Spirit,* Abingdon Press, 1975, pp. 13-14).

Christian reader, I invite you to join me in searching our hearts for attitudes and actions that quench the winds of the Spirit. We must be quickened for a fresh breath of the Holy Spirit to revive the church and reach the lost.

Prayer: O God, may Your Pentecostal gales blow across our churches until saints and sinners alike experience Your glorious presence once again!

Keep us on our knees in solemn assemblies until we surrender to the Sovereignty of Your Holy Spirit and make up our minds that we will not live another day without His fullness. Keep us before You until we are prepared for the greatest revival in the history of the church.

And, please, Lord, let this revival begin in me. Amen!

8

The Fire of the Spirit

Jesus said, *"I have come to bring fire on the earth, and how I wish it were already kindled"* (Luke 12:49).

John the Baptist said, *"I baptize you with water for repentance. But after me will come one who is more powerful than I, whose sandals I am not fit to carry. He will baptize you with the Holy Spirit and with fire. His winnowing fork is in his hand, and he will clear his threshing floor, gathering his wheat into the barn and burning up the chaff with unquenchable fire"* (Matthew 3:11-12).

The apostle Paul instructed Timothy to *"fan into flame the gift of God, which is in you through the laying on of my hands. For God did not give us a spirit of timidity, but a spirit of power, of love and of self-discipline"* (II Timothy 1:6-7).

Let us not discount the importance of fire as a symbol of the nature and work of the Holy Spirit in the life of God's children. Moses' initial personal experience with God began with his compelling interest in the burning bush. Throughout their wilderness pilgrimage the children of Israel were led by a pillar of fire.

Fire continues to be an important symbol in New Testament Christianity. Jesus Himself was anointed by the Holy Spirit before he went into public ministry. Who can read the four Gospels and deny that He burned with a holy fire in His praying, preaching, teaching, and working miracles? After His death and resurrection, and just before His ascension, He cited John's prophecy that He would baptize "with the Holy Spirit and with fire."

The Pentecostal outpouring marked a profound historical moment—the birth of the Church, the establishment of the New Covenant, and the Age of the Spirit. The giving of the Spirit was the fulfillment of the promise of the Father and the Son that true believers would be "clothed with power from on high" (Luke 24:49).

- *Refining fire*. The fire of the Holy Spirit is a *refining fire*. At Pentecost, and yet today, the filling of the Holy Spirit sanctifies the surrendered believer in a personal relationship with Jesus Christ for His Spirit to indwell richly and work powerfully in prayer, worship, and witness, as well as in an enablement for holy living. Two of Christ's apostles had sought places of power in a supposed political regime that He would head. But after the Pentecostal cleansing, we hear no more of their political ambitions. They now burned with a passion to glorify their Risen Lord—even suffering at the hands of those who had crucified Jesus. When threatened and forbidden to further preach Christ as Savior and Lord, Peter and John replied, "Judge for yourselves whether it is right in God's sight to obey you rather than God. For we cannot help speaking about what we have seen and heard" (Acts 4:19-20). The refining fire of the Spirit will enable us to deny self and obey the greatest of the commandments—"Love the Lord your God with all your heart and with all your soul and with all your strength and with all your mind; and, Love your neighbor as yourself" (Luke 10:27).

- *Radiating fire*. The fire of the Holy Spirit is a *radiating fire*. In their despairing defeat following Jesus' crucifixion, two doubting disciples met with the Risen Christ on the Emmaus Road. After talking with Him, they urged Him to remain and eat with them. When He had departed they asked each other, "Were not our hearts burning within us while he talked with us on the road and opened the Scriptures to us"

(Luke 24:32). The apostle James sensed the need of fire in our praying when he wrote, "The effectual fervent prayer of a righteous man availeth much" (James 5:16, KJV). Let us not be afraid of the passion of love when witnessing for Jesus Christ or worshiping or praying.

- *Rekindling fire.* We are commanded in the Word to see that the Holy Spirit is *a rekindling fire.* We are warned by the apostle Paul, "Do not put out the Spirit's fire" (I Thessalonians 5:19). The Spirit within us can be grieved, quenched, disobeyed, and ignored until He is forced by our free agency to slip into an inoperable mode, awaiting our repentance and restoration to His radiating presence. The imperial command, "Be filled with the Spirit" given by the apostle Paul in Ephesians 5:18 should read "Keep on being filled with the Spirit." While all truly born-again believers receive the Spirit in the moment of the new birth, this does not mean that they have reached the fullness of the Spirit. Many believers today are like some members of the church at Ephesus who had let the fire go out. Jesus warned, "I hold this against you: You have forsaken your first love. Remember the height from which you have fallen! Repent and do the things you did at first. If you do not repent, I will come to you and remove your lampstand from its place" (Revelation 2:4-5).

I will confess that there have been times in my nearly seven decades as a Christian believer when I have fallen short of the will of God and have gone before the Lord confessing with the psalmist: "Create in me a pure heart, O God, and renew a steadfast spirit within me. Do not cast me from your presence or take your Holy Spirit from me. Restore to me the joy of your salvation and grant me a willing spirit, to sustain me" (Psalm 51:10-12).

Coldhearted Christians cannot please the Lord, worship with passion, or win their loved ones and friends to Jesus Christ. Dear brothers and sisters, let us not go on living in apathy, deadness, blindness, emptiness, and powerlessness. No matter what or who the devil has used to maneuver you into your state of undoneness, the Holy Spirit is calling you back to His fire. It is not a wild fire! It is not a fanatical fire! It is not a freakish fire! It is a holy fire—redeeming, refining, radiating, and renewing.

I love a promise in Luke 11:13 that Jesus gives those who are serious about receiving the fullness of the Holy Spirit: "If you then, though you are evil, know how to give good gifts to your children, how much more will your Father in heaven give the Holy Spirit to those who ask him!"

Prayer: O God, forgive my spiritual coldness, my neglect of prayer, my hardness of heart. Please, Lord, I don't want to go on walking afar off from You. My heart longs for communion with You, the warmth and reassurance of Your presence, and the fire of Your power in my praying, worshiping, and witnessing. Forgive me for neglecting Your Word. I know my cold heart grieves You, and I repent of this emptiness that I have allowed.

I've made up my mind that I don't want to go on in my cold, casual, callous way. I want the fire, freedom, and fullness of the Holy Spirit. Lord, You promised that if we would ask, we would receive; if we would seek, we would find; and if we would knock, the door would be opened to us. So I come asking, seeking, and knocking! I will not stop seeking until I have the fullness, freedom, and fervency of the fire You promised those who would ask! Please, Lord, give it to me now! Amen!

9

The Spirit of Revival

"The hand of the Lord was upon me, and he brought me out by the Spirit of the Lord and set me in the middle of a valley; it was full of bones. He led me back and forth among them, and I saw a great many bones on the floor of the valley, bones that were very dry. He asked me, 'Son of man, can these bones live?'

"I said, 'O Sovereign Lord, you alone know.'

"Then he said to me, 'Prophesy to these bones and say to them, Dry bones, hear the word of the Lord! This is what the Sovereign Lord says to these bones: I will make breath enter you, and you will come to life . . . . Then you will know that I am the Lord.'

"So I prophesied as I was commanded. And as I was prophesying, there was a noise, a rattling sound, and the bones came together, bone to bone. I looked, and tendons and flesh appeared on them and skin covered them, but there was no breath in them.

"Then he said to me, 'Prophesy to the breath; prophesy, son of man, and say to it, This is what the Sovereign Lord says: Come from the four winds, O breath, and breathe into these slain, that they may live.'

"So I prophesied as He commanded me, and breath entered them; they came to life and stood up on their feet—a vast army" (Ezekiel 37:1-10).

Ezekiel was led into a valley where long ago a mighty battle had left hundreds of thousands slaughtered. No one had survived to bury the dead. Vultures had long since picked the carcasses clean, and there were the bones. The rains of the centuries had washed them thin, and a thousand summer suns had bleached them white as snow. It was a dismal scene. The prophet saw that the bones were very dry.

There was to be no misunderstanding about the meaning of the vision. God said to the prophet, "Son of man, these bones are the whole house of Israel" (Ezekiel 37:11). Their bones were dry, their hope was gone, and they had been cut off. And God definitely means Israel!

The strange cycle of the backsliding of the people of God across the ages is a very haunting phenomenon. Israel represented the people of God in Old Testament times. They often failed to meet the conditions of their covenant with Jehovah, and the resulting apostasy wrote tragedy into their history. Judgment must come on the disobedient!

For over two millennia under the New Covenant, Christians through their disobedience are just as guilty of grieving the Holy Spirit as were the Israelites. Like it or not, Ezekiel's valley of dry bones is a striking symbol of paralyzed churches and powerless Christians in our time—lifeless, paralyzed, and hopeless, except for the one source that God offered the prophet for reviving the bones—*the wind of the Spirit*.

American Christians number in the millions, but the smell of death is on many of our churches. We are too dead to hunger and thirst for either the meat or milk of the Word, too lifeless in our worship and praise of the God who sent His only Son to die for our sins, and too busy to stop and think about our need to prevail with God in prayer. *Nothing can revive us except the wind of the Spirit.*

The Lord asked the prophet, "Son of man, can these bones live?" In other words, "Do you really believe that I can transform this appalling valley of death into a garden of glory and life again?" The prophet was being tested, just as the Spirit of God is testing believers in every community in our land today. Do we believe in the God of the supernatural? Do we believe He can still work miracles? The world is full of venturesome people who believe in the possible. God is looking for believers who will believe in the God of the impossible.

When Ezekiel showed himself ready to obey God and to see the miracle, he was given two commands, "Prophesy to these bones and say to them, 'Dry bones, hear the word of the Lord!'" (v. 4); and "Prophesy to the breath *(the wind)* . . . and say to it . . . 'Come from the four winds, O breath, and breathe into these slain, that they may live'" (v. 9). Prophesying to the wind for Ezekiel is tantamount to our praying to the Holy Spirit today to bring new life to His people. The Old Testament promise is valid and binding on Christian believers today: "If my people, who are called by my name, will humble themselves and pray and seek my face and turn from their wicked ways, then will I hear from heaven and will forgive their sin and will heal their land" (II Chronicles 7:14).

Even as Ezekiel was preaching to the bones, "there was a noise, a rattling sound, and the bones came together, bone to bone . . . tendons and flesh appeared on them and skin covered them, but there was no breath in them" (vv. 7-8). Not yet!

That a miracle had happened there was no denying. But the prophet had followed the Spirit and the Word too closely to mistake appearances, noise, and movements for true revival. The situation fell short of what God had promised. Mere movement among the bones was not the answer, so he kept on preaching and praying until there were true signs of life.

"So I prophesied as he commanded me, and breath entered them; they came to life and stood up on their feet—a vast army" (v. 10). Here at last was what God had promised and what the prophet had prayed for—a people filled with the Spirit of Jesus Christ; filled with love, joy, and peace; liberated for worship, praise, and holy living; and empowered to witness to a lost world.

Can we allow God, who came in power on the 120 believers in the Upper Room so long ago and empowered them to go out and turn their world right side up, to come upon us today with the same wind and fire that can transform lifeless Christians into a living, marching army? Only a mighty moving of the Spirit can transform us into radiant believers who will attract our children, grandchildren, and neighbors to Jesus Christ. Only a rekindling of the Spirit's fire can cause our churches to be aflame in spiritual life and capture the interest of our communities.

But this revival has to start with individuals—you and me. Are we ready to dare to tell God, "Lord, I'll not remain in a powerless profession of grace and my state of deadness and emptiness; I'm ready to take seriously your promise in Luke 11:13." You said, 'If you . . . know how to give good gifts to your children, how much more will your Father in heaven give the Holy Spirit to those who ask him.'"

Prayer: Lord, I confess my need of revival. I humble myself before you, acknowledging my selfishness, worldliness, and slowness to obey Your Word. Forgive my neglect of prayer and fervent worship. I believe it is time for me to seek Your face—Your favor, Your fellowship, Your renewed blessing on my life. I've been so anxious to please others and to have this or that more so than Your will and way in my life. Enable me to die out to my wishes and wants that are truly unimportant compared to getting back into the center of Your will.

Lord, it is time for me to "turn from (my) wicked ways"—my prayerlessness, my selfishness, my insincere worship, my neglect of Your Word, my negative thinking, my critical spirit, my complaining, my unbelief. Please, Lord, show me other sins I need to confess. I ask Your forgiveness and believe Your Word that You do forgive me and cleanse me from all unrighteousness.

Fill me with Your Holy Spirit, Lord! Yes, come in fullness, freedom, and power! I'm tired of my deadness and emptiness; I must live in the power You promised and know that the winds of the Spirit are blowing daily in my life!

Thank You, Lord, for the stirring of Your Spirit in my life to be restored to Your grace and power. Amen!

10

The Spirit of Truth

"If you love me, you will obey what I command. And I will ask the Father, and he will give you another Counselor to be with you forever—the Spirit of truth . . ." (John 14:15-17).

It appears that Jesus' favorite title for the Holy Spirit is "The Spirit of truth." Since Jesus declared himself to be "the truth" (John 14:6), we should not be surprised that He would refer to His successor, His alter ego, His very Spirit, as "the Spirit of truth."

The human race was led astray by a deceiver, a bold liar, in the Garden of Eden. The master deceiver has been leading people astray for thousands of years. When he fell from Heaven, he lost his holiness but not his craftiness. In the Garden of Eden, we read of the devil's skill and guile in deceiving Eve. The apostle Paul warned the Corinthians, "I am afraid that just as Eve was deceived by the serpent's cunning, your minds may somehow be led astray from your sincere and pure devotion to Christ" (II Corinthians 11:3).

God gave His "one and only Son" (John 3:16) to rescue us from sin and evil. Jesus declared Himself to be "the way and the truth and the life" (John 14:6). But even our Lord became a target of the evil one. Satan schemed to defeat God's mission of redemption of the human race by trying to distract Jesus from His atoning death on the cross.

Satan's first line of attack is usually through the mind. Satan has access to our thought life and is allowed to influence our thinking by sometimes prompting thoughts of self-pity or attempting to cause us to exaggerate offenses we have suffered and to brood over our hurts and needs. How tragic that so many Christians fail to discern the source of their thoughts that are leading them right into the devil's trap of spiritual defeat. Of course, the enemy never announces, "This is the devil speaking."

Jesus had been anointed of the Holy Spirit at His baptism, and then was led by the Spirit into the wilderness of temptation. Sitting there hungry, having fasted 40 days and 40 nights, He needed something to eat. A thought came to Him of turning stones into bread to satisfy His hunger. But His sensitivity to the Holy Spirit prompted our Lord to discern the source of His thinking—*the enemy is tempting me to use my special powers to satisfy my hunger!* Jesus fired back, "It is written: 'Man does not live on bread alone, but on every word that comes from the mouth of God'" (Matthew 4:4). Satan was defeated.

Again, Jesus was thinking about His role as the Messiah: perhaps only two people in all the world believed in Him—His Blessed Mother, Mary, and John the Baptist. How was He to gain a following? Thoughts came to Him about going to the Temple plaza and during a great feast leap down and land intact, thus impressing a following. Almost immediately Jesus recognized that the evil one had returned to mess with His mind. Again, he fired back, "It is also written, 'Do not put the Lord your God to the test'" (Matthew 4:7). Satan departed from Him.

But the evil one was determined to defeat our Lord. Jesus knew He had been born to become King of kings, and He knew He was to receive His kingdom from the Father in due time—not from the evil one and not now. All at once it seemed as if He were looking through a telescope of time seeing "all the kingdoms of the world" and a voice offering, "I will give you all their authority and splendor . . . if you worship me" (Luke 4:5-7). Jesus did not give it a second thought, but fired back, "It is written: 'Worship the Lord your God and serve him only'" (Luke 4:8). Satan was soundly defeated.

While we mortals are no match for the devil when it comes to temptation, we must remember that we are not alone. The Holy Spirit is *our Holy Guest*, living within us. Just think of it: The Holy Spirit is the very Spirit of God the Father and God the Son, who has come to indwell us! As we abide in Him, we have this glorious built-in warning when evil is near. We are given wisdom, courage, and direction as to how to deal with the devil when he tempts, threatens, and lies to us.

Then why do so many Christians go down in defeat? Because they do not allow the Spirit to lead them consistently for prayer, reading of the Word, and worship. When we grieve, quench, disobey, or ignore the Holy Spirit, He is left inoperative within us until we repent and are restored in fellowship with Him. Not only is our Heavenly Father the Light of the World, but Jesus Christ is also the Light of the World. Their Spirit lives in us to light up our way. From the human beginning in the Garden of Eden it was Satan's purpose to destroy the plan of God for Adam and Eve. His strategy was to bring about doubt of God's Word to them. He managed to succeed in causing Eve to doubt so that she would disobey and partake of the forbidden fruit, eventually causing Adam to compromise.

The evil one continues to lie to believers today about God's work, God's purposes, and God's will for us. If he tried to throw Jesus off His mission to save us, be assured he will not give up easily on causing us to make shipwreck of our faith.

So, what is our secret to defeating Satan? *Prayerfully discerning the truth from the Holy Spirit!* This usually comes from the Scriptures more often than from the counsel of wiser and older believers. Remember, Jesus had been *anointed* by the Holy Spirit before Satan's attack. When he discerned the source of His thoughts of temptation, He answered Satan with quotes from the Word of God. The Holy Spirit is the Spirit of truth, and the Holy Bible is the Word of truth. We must learn to trust the Spirit's revealing the Word of truth to us. "The Spirit searches all things, even the deep things of God. For who among men knows the thoughts of a man except the man's spirit within him? In the same way no one knows the thoughts of God except the Spirit of God. We have not received the spirit of the world but the spirit who is from God, that we may understand what God has freely given us" (I Corinthians 2:10-12). Only with the Holy Spirit within us as our illuminator can we gain such intimate knowledge of Christ. We can know the glory of His presence, the purity of His mind, the depth of His joy, the yearning of His love, the beauty of His will, and the fullness of His power.

If we are truly born-again children of God who are serious about God's will for our lives, our most reliable source for keeping on the straight-and-narrow way is found in learning to obey the Holy

Spirit. I've learned that the Spirit will sometimes guide us through one or more of the following ways: (1) A definite conviction formed while studying a passage of Scripture, (2) The prayerful and dutiful exercise of common sense, (3) The Spirit-regulated influence of conscience, (4) The counsel of other mature and gifted believers, (5) The open and closed doors of circumstances, (6) The prophetic utterances from a Spirit-filled brother or sister, and (7) A word of knowledge tested in prayer by "trying the spirits."

Something should be said about *obeying* God's will after we find out what it is. Discovering the will of God is often easier than *doing* it. When the will of God includes suffering (self-denial)—and it often does—how are we to delight in it and joyfully obey it? The answer is still the same: We must rely as much on the help of the Holy Spirit for strengthening us to obey as we did for enlightening us in the first place. The apostle Paul instructed believers, "work out your own salvation with fear and trembling; for it is God who works in you both to will and to do for *His* good pleasure" (Philippians 2:12-13, NKJV).

Prayer: Thank You, Lord, for saving me, adopting me into Your family, and giving me the Gift of Your Holy Spirit, the Spirit of Truth. O God, help me realize more seriously the need to walk in ungrieved fellowship with Your Holy Spirit so as to maintain devotion, inspiration, and a sense of Your presence.

Forgive my times of running past the checks of the Spirit, neglecting the Word of God, and procrastinating the urgent calls of the Spirit to pray. I do confess that by my neglect I have smothered or quenched the Spirit at times.

Please, Lord, rekindle the fires of the Spirit. Saturate me with the oil of the Spirit that I might be the flame You want me to be in these dark and troubled times. Forbid that I fail to obey the Spirit of truth. Amen!

11

The Spirit of Light

"The Spirit searches all things, even the deep things of God. For who among men knows the thoughts of a man except the man's spirit within him? In the same way no one knows the thoughts of God except the Spirit of God. We have not received the spirit of the world but the Spirit who is from God, that we may understand what God has freely given us. This is what we speak, not in words taught us by human wisdom but in words taught by the Spirit, expressing spiritual truths in spiritual words. The man without the Spirit does not accept the things that come from the Spirit of God, for they are foolishness to him, and he cannot understand them, because they are spiritually discerned" (I Corinthians 2:10-14).

Just as Jesus was the Spirit of truth so His Spirit is the Spirit of truth. And just as Jesus is "the light of the world" (John 8:12), so His Spirit is the Spirit of light—the Spirit of illumination so that the Christian believer can find his way.

Pastor David Jeremiah tells the story of his friend's visit to Romania just months after the fall of the wicked tyrant Nicolae Ceausescu. Even with the insane dictator gone, Bucharest was a dreary capital city and bullet holes scarred the walls of many of its buildings. It was actually a nation filled with darkness, because commodities such as light bulbs were simply unavailable in the country at that time. The man was staying in an apartment in one of the massive cement complexes. He got out of a taxicab and tried to remember where his apartment was. But it was an extremely dark night—no streetlights, no lights in the windows—with an oppressive evil in the air. He got into an elevator in what he hoped was the right building. The elevator had no lighting, encasing him in a box of utter darkness. Was someone else in the elevator? He felt for where the panel might be, found only a few buttons, and pushed one and hoped it would take him to the third floor. The door opened to another level of deepest night. He groped his way along, wondering if he was being followed; he was tempted to panic and scream. He began feeling for numbers on the doors, wishing he had even a penlight—what a difference that even a flashlight would make!

We live in a fallen, darkened world. We ourselves walked in darkness before we found Jesus Christ as our light. But once we have trusted in Jesus as our Savior, we do not walk in darkness. "For you were once darkness, but now you are light in the Lord. Live as children of light (for the fruit of the light consists in all goodness, righteousness and truth) and find out what pleases the Lord" (Ephesians 5:8-10).

When we are born again we receive the gift of the Holy Spirit. We don't ask for Him; the Spirit is an essential part of the miracle of the new birth. We soon discover Him with the new interests that come for communion with God in prayer, an appetite for the Word of God, a yearning to praise and worship God, and a need to fellowship with other believers and become a part of the body of Christ.

I could hardly believe the difference my conversion to Christ made in my wanting to study the Bible. As an unbeliever, I had given up on understanding the Bible; it made little sense to me. When I became a believer in Jesus, I discovered not just a hunger for the Scriptures; there was also light and understanding and real meaning in what I read. The Holy Spirit made the difference. The same Holy Spirit who inspired the writers of our Bible is present with true believers to illumine us as we read those same truths today.

We have assurance from the apostle John that believers have an advantage over the natural man—the person who has not been born again. He writes, "But you have an anointing from the Holy One, and all of you know the truth" (I John 2:20). John means that all true believers have an indwelling Helper who sheds light on the Scriptures they read and study. He, the Holy Spirit, who inspired the writer to write will also inspire the reader who reads. The Spirit will shed light on the meaning the author sought to convey when he wrote it. Even though sin had darkened our understanding, when we come to Christ as Savior, we are blessed to have access to the light of the Word of God and the advantage of our indwelling Guest's illumination. So we have no excuse for walking in darkness.

The apostle Paul commands, "Live by the Spirit, and you will not gratify the desires of the sinful nature. For the sinful nature desires what is contrary to the Spirit, and the Spirit what is contrary to the sinful nature" (Galatians 5:16-17). I am not being paranoid when I declare that we born-again Christians have someone on our trails determined to confuse, frustrate, defeat, and ensnare. Satan is a deceiver and will go any distance to undermine God's purpose for us. But let us take it straight from the Word of God what that purpose is: "For those God foreknew he also predestined to be conformed to the likeness of his Son" (Romans 8:29). The same apostle tells us how this is done as we "live by the Spirit. And we, who with unveiled faces all reflect the Lord's glory, are being transformed into his likeness with ever-increasing glory, which comes from the Lord, who is the Spirit" (II Corinthians 3:18). If we aren't yet as Christlike as we know we need to be, we are to sincerely continue to open our hearts to Jesus; confess our sins, failures, and shortcomings; and hold steady in surrender to Him. His very Spirit will increase our knowledge *of* Him, purify our faith *in* Him, and deepen our love *for* Him. We are children of the God of light—His Spirit shines His love, life, and light in our hearts. By the Spirit we radiate His love and grace to the people in darkness in a way that the Spirit will make them hungry for the same qualities they see in us.

The Word of God is telling us here that if we will obey the Spirit and continue to look to Jesus, we'll be given power through the Spirit to live in holiness and grace and not succumb to the temptations of our enemy, the devil. One victory over temptation should lead to another victory until we become totally convinced that we are enabled by the Spirit to live in obedience to God. When we are tempted, we can only survive victoriously as we, by the Spirit, say no to those temptations to please any selfish desire (Romans 8:13).

Jesus sought to impress on Nicodemus the required commitment of following through with the believer's profession of faith in Christ when He said, "whoever lives by the truth comes into the light" (John 3:21). Our walking with Christ will mean that we are walking in moral and spiritual light, no longer yielding to the darkness of selfishness and sin. Our life is not only fulfilling to us personally but it is also appealing to others, causing them to be interested concerning our inner resources for a life that satisfies.

Jesus tells us that He expects His light to be reflected in our lives in order that we might reach others so that they can experience all that we have known in Him. He says, "You are the light of the world. A city on a hill cannot be hidden. Neither do people light a lamp and put it under a bowl. Instead they put it on its stand, and it gives light to everyone in the house. In the same way, let your light shine before men, that they may see your good deeds and praise your Father in heaven" (Matthew 5:14-16). We need to allow our light to be seen in deeds and words, but for the right purpose—giving praise to the One who has changed us and shines His love through us.

Prayer: Lord, forgive me for the times when my selfish conduct has shaded the light of Your glory and caused others to say, "If that's Christianity, I want no part of it." Holy Spirit, cleanse me and enable me to deny myself when I'm tempted to contend for my way and gain attention to myself. Lord, I want to be close enough to You to obey Your Word that tells me that You oppose the proud but give grace to the humble. So help me submit myself to You and resist the devil so he will flee from me. Then I can draw near You and You will draw near to me (James 4:6-8).

Give me courage and wisdom for letting my light shine in the presence of family, friends, and people of the world. I do want to be winsome for You. I realize that You have called me to be a witness to the saved and to the lost. I pray for grace to come out of the shadows. Give me a holy boldness to speak out and shine out for You. Amen!

12

The Spirit of Thanksgiving

"... be filled with the Spirit. Speak to one another with psalms, hymns and spiritual songs. Sing and make music in your heart to the Lord, always giving thanks to God the Father for everything, in the name of our Lord Jesus Christ" (Ephesians 5:18-20).

"Let the peace of Christ rule in your hearts, since as members of one body you were called to peace. And be thankful. Let the word of Christ dwell in you richly as you teach and admonish one another with all wisdom, and as you sing psalms, hymns, and spiritual songs with gratitude in your hearts to God. And whatever you do, whether in word or deed, do it all in the name of the Lord Jesus, giving thanks to God the Father through him" (Colossians 3:15-17).

All born-again believers receive the gift of the Holy Spirit when they respond to the Gospel of Jesus Christ in sincere repentance and a confession of faith (Acts 2:38-39, Romans 8:9, II Corinthians 1:21, II Corinthians 5:5, Galatians 3:1-5, Ephesians 1:13-14, Titus 3:4-6).

But we must realize that not all believers who have the Holy Spirit are *filled* with the Spirit. Some are carnal, careless, disobedient, and downright selfish, ignoring the Spirit within them and the Scriptures they read. But, according to our New Testament, a strong evidence of being filled with the Spirit is *an attitude of gratitude*. No, the attitude of gratitude is not the only evidence of a Spirit-filled believer, but it is a prominent proof that the Spirit fills the believing heart.

Since Spirit-filled Christians are worshipers, thanksgiving should be a major part of our worship. When the Holy Spirit is given control of our minds, hearts, and time, we cease the negative thinking that gives rise to doubting, worrying, complaining, judging, whining, accusing, coveting, and self-pitying. The apostle Paul admonishes, "Let the peace of Christ rule in your hearts . . . and be thankful." Such believers can sing God's praises and offer up sacrifices to the Lord in spiritual songs of gratitude that might well be poured out most of the day and into the night. Such acts of worship would certainly cover a "multitude of sins!" The same Holy Spirit who helps us worship God creates the peace in our hearts, and from that peace flows a thankful heart.

When the psalmist caught himself in sadness and despair, he addressed his own inner person, "Why are you downcast, O my soul? Why so disturbed within me? Put your hope in God, for I will yet praise him, my Savior and my God . . ." (Psalm 42:5-6). We sometimes need the courage to speak to our inner person and then wait on the Lord for some answers as to our negative thinking. We must recognize lowness of spirit and lack of being grateful to God for His manifold blessings as abnormal for believers. These conditions rob us of our fellowship with God. It is a sin for Christians to go on for hours and even days without breaking out in genuine heartfelt praise and thanksgiving to God for salvation and for physical, spiritual, financial, and relational blessings.

I need to confess that there have been periods in my life when I've gone too long without praising and thanking the Lord for His grace and mercies. In preparing my heart to recover, I've repented of the pride and self-consciousness that led to the absence of the spirit of thankfulness that should have been flowing from my heart and lips. I'm learning that the indwelling Holy Spirit is grieved when we allow Satan to manipulate our stream of self-consciousness to cross the line into self-pity, self-protection, and self-worship. It's no wonder that Jesus warned that our enemy is a robber, and that he "comes only to steal and kill and destroy" (John 10:10). Satan doesn't need to target the unbeliever in such a way; however, he so hates and fears the

Spirit-filled believer that we are under his constant attack.

We must not ignore the command that the apostle Paul gave the Colossian believers: "And whatever you do, whether in word or deed, do it all in the name of the Lord Jesus, giving thanks to God the Father through him." To the believers at Ephesus he insisted that thanksgiving should be "always" and "for everything." These instructions holding Christians to thanksgiving *for everything* come from an apostle who spent time in prison, endured beating and stoning, and often faced death. But, if we pay close attention to his New Testament writings, we'll see that he practiced what he preached.

Americans should read the warning God's Word gave to a people that arrogantly closed their minds and hearts to any accountability to Almighty God. That nation or community continued to sink deeper and deeper into the swamps of its own sick behavior. Listen to how the apostle describes it: "For although they knew God, they neither glorified him as God nor gave thanks to him, but their thinking became futile and their foolish hearts were darkened. Although they claimed to be wise, they became fools" (Romans 1:21-22). Are Americans today being described in this passage? God forbid that we professing Christians omit thanksgiving in our public worship and private devotions! If we have ceased being thankful, then we must seek a fresh filling of the Spirit in order to recapture the sincere practice of thanksgiving in all things!

Our God is not only our Creator; He is our Savior, Provider, Healer, Comforter, Counselor, Convicter, and Cleanser from sin. In order to recover from the sin of ingratitude, we must begin with confession of that sin.

Prayer: Father God, forgive my sin of ingratitude. Forgive my tendency to be without deep feelings when I utter expressions of thanksgiving.

Heavenly Father, You suffered beyond anything we mortals can imagine when You sacrificed Your one and only Son to die an atoning death on Calvary's cross for our sins. Lord Jesus, You suffered far beyond anything we humans can understand when You emptied Yourself of the glory of Your exalted place in Heaven with the Holy Trinity. Even as You retained Your deity as the Son of Man here on earth, You laid aside the splendor of the transcendent attributes of divinity in order to become one with us. You suffered rejection, persecution, and accusations by those who claimed to be righteous as well as by those who knew they were evil. But in paying the ultimate price for our salvation, You suffered pain and shame and the most ignominious death anyone ever endured! Lord Jesus, forgive our casual expressions, our nonchalant forms, our cheap efforts of worship. O, Savior, give us passionate, worshipful hearts of thanksgiving. In seeking to worship You in expressions of thanksgiving, we are reminded that when King David felt compelled to offer a sacrifice to God and needed a place to offer it, he declined the generosity of a wealthy landowner who wished to provide both the sacrifice and his threshing floor. And the king refused by saying, "No, I insist on paying the full price. I will not take for the Lord what is yours, or sacrifice a burnt offering that costs me nothing" (I Chronicles 21:24).

Lord, forgive my cheap worship. Sometimes I've excused myself from offering up the sacrifices of praise and thanksgiving because I felt too weary, too busy, or too bothered by other things. I've only allowed this to happen for one reason—I had fallen into the habit of ignoring the constraints of the Holy Spirit and settled for cheap worship.

And, Lord, how do I recover from cheap worship? Thank You for Your Word: "If we confess our sins, he is faithful and just and will forgive us our sins and purify us from all unrighteousness" (I John 1:9). Thank You, Holy Spirit, for convicting me of my sin of ingratitude. Help me, lest I fall into the Slough of Despond and again begin the miserable effort to walk in cheap grace, not willing to offer myself as a living sacrifice.

Father God, from here on I seek, with Your help, to walk in fellowship with an ungrieved, unquenched, unignored Holy Spirit and in all things be thankful. Amen!

13

The Spirit of Conviction

"Nevertheless I tell you the truth. It is to your advantage that I go away; for if I do not go away, the Helper will not come to you; but if I depart, I will send Him to you. And when He has come, He will convict the world of sin, and of righteousness, and of judgment: of sin, because they do not believe in Me; of righteousness, because I go to My Father and you see Me no more; of judgment, because the ruler of this world is judged" (John 16:7-11, NKJV).

Jesus prepared His disciples for His departure, promising to send the Holy Spirit to work in redeeming power in their lives and ministries just as He had allowed the Holy Spirit to work in His life and ministry.

The Holy Spirit is the Spirit of Salvation. No one can be saved apart from the work of the Holy Spirit. We will never realize our sinfulness until we are convicted (convinced) of sin. Certainly, we cannot confess that we are sinners unless the Spirit does His work within us. Even our confession of Christ as Savior is not possible unless there is convincing by the Spirit to our needy heart that He truly is the Son of God. The apostle Paul wrote, "no one can say, 'Jesus is Lord,' except by the Holy Spirit" (I Corinthians 12:3). The natural human heart must be penetrated by the Holy Spirit in conviction before we are convinced of our need of spiritual regeneration. Previous to this gracious work of the Spirit we are prone to argue that we will gain heaven by our good works. It was shocking news to Nicodemus when Jesus told the great theologian, "You must be born again" (John 3:7).

Jesus made it clear that the convicting work of the Holy Spirit would have to do with at least three things: *sin, righteousness, and judgment.*

- *Conviction regarding sin.* The Holy Spirit penetrates the heart and mind of the sinner to combat self-righteousness and prove us guilty of sin. Only as we acknowledge this to be true and confess Jesus Christ as our Lord and Savior can we be saved. But we need to be reminded that it is the Spirit of God who makes it clear to us that we are lost, sinful, and undeserving of eternal life and that only by believing in Christ can we be saved. Jesus goes on to make unbelief the prime example of sin when He says, "in regard to sin, because men do not believe in me" (John 16:9). Failure to believe in Jesus Christ as mankind's only Savior is the greatest sin. Jesus made this clear to Nicodemus when He said, "God did not send his Son into the world to condemn the world, but to save the world through him. Whoever believes in him is not condemned, but whoever does not believe stands condemned already because he has not believed in the name of God's one and only Son" (John 3:17-18).

- *Conviction regarding righteousness.* Christian believers need to consider the gracious work of salvation accomplished by God in establishing the righteousness available to the believer by the sacrificial death of Jesus Christ on Calvary's cross. There is an infinite distance between the righteousness of Jesus Christ and the lostness of sinners for whom Christ died on the cross. He, the holy and righteous One, died for us vicariously, the just for the unjust. "God made him who had no sin to be sin for us, so that in him we might become the righteousness of God" (II Corinthians 5:21). Jesus Christ's resurrection and then His ascension to the right hand of God the Father established Him as the absolute standard for righteousness. And the Holy Spirit will convince us of our just status before God when we have trusted in Jesus Christ alone for our salvation. "Therefore, since we have been justified through faith, we have peace with God through our Lord Jesus Christ, through whom we have gained access by faith into this grace in which we now stand. And we rejoice in the hope of the glory of God" (Romans 5:1-2). In our new birth, the Holy Spirit *imputes* to us the righteousness of Christ; in sanctification, the Holy Spirit *imparts* to us the righteousness of Christ, enabling us to live out the Christ-like qualities—the fruit of the Spirit: "love, joy, peace, patience, kindness, goodness, faithfulness, gentleness and self-control" (Galatians 5:22-23).

- *Conviction regarding judgment.* The death of Jesus Christ on the cross became the utter condemnation and defeat of sin. The Christian believer is forgiven, born again, and indwelt by the Spirit's power for living the Christian life. The same Holy Spirit seeks to keep us conscious of the coming "judgment seat of Christ" (II Corinthians 5:10) at which "we must all appear . . . that each one may receive what is due him for the things done while in the body, whether good or bad." We must realize that this is a judgment at which only believers appear. Our accountability to our Lord will be a serious and solemn meeting. And for a time, there will be sadness and tears for disobedience—for which we sought forgiveness—but we'll be called to face up to the consequences, which will mean a lesser reward. Remember, the Judgment Seat of Christ is not a judgment to determine who goes to Heaven or to Hell, but it is for believers who are all going to Heaven because they have believed the blood of Jesus Christ paid for their sins and they have been forgiven; they will not be condemned. This judgment is to determine their valued works of righteousness during their Christian life on earth.

Unbelievers will face the Great White Throne Judgment (Revelation 20:11-15). This is not a judgment to determine whether they go to Heaven or to Hell. All in this judgment will go to Hell, because their names are "not found written in the book of life", and they are "thrown into the lake of fire" (v. 15). Little wonder that Christ commissioned His church to proclaim His Gospel to the ends of the earth so that sinners ("whosoever will") might be saved and assured of eternal life with our Lord forever!

But we also read of the judgment Satan will ultimately receive: "And the devil, who deceived them, was thrown into the lake of burning sulfur, where the beast and the false prophet had been thrown. They will be tormented day and night for ever and ever" (Revelation 20:10). Satan has known from the moment of his rebellion and abandonment from Heaven that he is doomed for an eternal Hell. Yet he is given the freedom to roam the world and seek to prevent the glory of God and to blind the minds of humanity to the Gospel of Jesus Christ lest they believe and be saved. He attempts to hinder believers in their Christian duties of praying, worshiping, witnessing, and living a life of holiness and power. He is also free to strategize against those believers who seek to wage spiritual warfare against his evil kingdom.

Prayer: O God, thank You for giving me Your Holy Spirit. How I long to live and walk in holy fellowship with an ungrieved, unquenched, Holy Spirit! I'm grateful for Your faithfulness to convict me of the times when I fall short of Your glory and when I grow careless, selfish, lazy, and insensitive to Your will for me. I want to maintain the Spirit's fullness, fire, and freedom and consistently bear the fruit of the Spirit. I am so grateful, Lord, for the Spirit's faithful warnings when I'm failing to abide in the Word and not allowing the Word to abide in me. Yes, I confess, Lord, there have been times when I've sensed a withering of my relationship with You. Thank You for Your forgiveness when I have confessed my sin of neglect. How I praise You for Your merciful renewing and refilling of the Spirit!

With the psalmist I have learned that I can pray, "Create in me a pure heart, O God, and renew a steadfast spirit within me. Do not cast me from your presence or take your Holy Spirit from me. Restore to me the joy of your salvation and grant me a willing spirit, to sustain me" (Psalm 51:10-12).

Lord, I want to be in daily readiness for detecting instantly the Spirit's constraints or restraints. Oh, to be obedient, to be filled with praise and worship, and to be ready to witness or carry out any assignment You would give me. Help me not to be afraid to offer You my "body as a living sacrifice, holy and pleasing"—and may I do this as a true act of spiritual worship. May I "not conform any longer to the pattern of this world, but be transformed by the renewing of (my)mind" that I might be "able to test and approve what God's will is—his good, pleasing and perfect will" (Romans 12:1-2). Amen!

14

The Spirit of Assurance

"... those who are led by the Spirit of God are sons of God. For you did not receive a spirit that makes you a slave again to fear, but you received the Spirit of sonship. And by him we cry 'Abba, Father.' The Spirit himself testifies with our spirit that we are God's children. Now if we are children, then we are heirs—heirs of God and co-heirs with Christ, if indeed we share in his sufferings in order that we may also share in his glory" (Romans 8:14-17).

Evangelical Christians are known for their certainty of salvation. As my mother, Estelle, used to say, "I have a *know-so* salvation. I know that I have eternal life, and I know that Jesus lives in my heart and that when I die I'm going to heaven."

Estelle Tharp did not gain her certainty of salvation from the evangelist from whom she heard the Gospel and believed. She did not get her assurance of salvation from a book on theology. The Holy Spirit Himself testified with her spirit that she was a child of God!

Actually, all true believers receive the Holy Spirit when they are born again. The apostle Paul wrote, "And you also were included in Christ when you heard the word of truth, the gospel of your salvation. Having believed, you were marked in him (Christ) with a seal, the promised Holy Spirit, who is a deposit guaranteeing our inheritance until the redemption of those who are God's possession—to the praise of his glory" (Ephesians 1:13-14).

• *Sonship*. All human beings are children of God by creation. But only those who believe in God's one and only Son become His redeemed children. Actually, Jesus shocked and angered the unbelieving Pharisees who wanted to kill Him by telling them, "You belong to your father, the devil" (John 8:44). They were rejecting God's only prescribed Savior. They were slaves to the very nature of the devil and sought to murder Jesus. The apostle Paul reminds believers that we all were once slaves to fear, but since believing we have "received the Spirit of sonship." And the Holy Spirit within us testifies to our born-again relationship with Jesus Christ and the Father. *"Abba, Father"* is an expression of an intimate relationship. As God's adopted children, our names are recorded in "the book of life" (Revelation 3:5, 13:8, 17:8, 20:12, 20:15). Millions of fathers and mothers across the world record their children's names in their Family Bible. But it seems that our Heavenly Father has His "Book of Life" for believers who are His adopted children. Jesus told His disciples to "rejoice that your names are written in heaven" (Luke 10:20).

• *Heirs*. Since we are no longer slaves to fear, but have become children of freedom as redeemed children of God, we are called to places and positions of responsibility. We are called "heirs of God and co-heirs with Christ, if indeed we share in his sufferings in order that we may also share in his glory." The Bible makes it clear again and again that the Father gives everything to the Son and that the Son shares His inheritance with us, His followers. Remaining in Christ, we are assured of a future entrance into our inheritance. Every believer has been given gifts for service to the Lord. We need to identify our spiritual gifts and prayerfully find our places to allow the expressions of our gifts. Christians who are serving the Lord with their gifts are blessed believers. Whether the spiritual gifts are teaching, preaching, healing, giving, helping, hospitality, or another one, the church body will be blessed richly as we obey the Spirit's leading in the expression of our gifts.

• *Freedom*. The apostle Paul wrote, "It is for freedom that Christ has set us free. Stand firm, then, and do not let yourselves be burdened again by a yoke of slavery" (Galatians 5:1). A Christian in bondage cannot be a good witness to the world, nor can he or she be a great blessing to the church. I've met people who were in bondage to people; they simply cannot be free around certain individuals. Some are in bondage to an unChristlike attitude; they can't seem to bear with difficult persons and manage to forgive them. Some are in bondage to religion; they feel condemned if they fail to measure up to the convictions or opinions of other respected Christians. The apostle Paul in writing the book of Galatians was seeking to show up the dangers of legalism—the belief that they would be saved by keeping the Law. Jesus said, "Now a slave has no permanent place in the family, but a son belongs to it forever. So if the Son sets you free, you will be free indeed" (John 8:35-36). A deeper life in the Spirit will bring freedom from the bondage of sin, the world, and selfishness. As we keep our eyes on Jesus, the Holy Spirit will help us become passionate worshipers, obedient followers, and faithful sons and daughters of God.

Prayer: Lord, I'm going to claim Your promise that "where the Spirit of the Lord is, there is freedom" (II Corinthians 3:17). Help me to concentrate so intensely on the glory of Jesus that I am being transformed continuously into His likeness with the ever-increasing glory that comes from the Spirit within me.

Thank You, Lord, for filling me with Your Spirit, who assures me of Your abiding presence and a place with You throughout eternity. Amen!

15

The Sins Against the Spirit

"And do not grieve the Holy Spirit of God, by whom you were sealed for the day of redemption. Let all bitterness, wrath, anger, clamor, and evil speaking be put away from you, with all malice. And be kind to one another, tenderhearted, forgiving one another, just as God in Christ also forgave you" (Ephesians 4:30-32, NKJV).

"But Peter said, 'Ananias, why has Satan filled your heart to lie to the Holy Spirit and keep back a part of the price of the land for yourself? While it remained, was it not your own? And after it was sold, was it not in your own control? Why have you conceived this thing in your heart? You have not lied to men but to God'" (Acts 5:3-4, NKJV).

"Do not put out the Spirit's fire" (I Thessalonians 5:19).

Many religions acknowledge God as Spirit, but only Christianity sets forth the doctrine of the Holy Spirit as a personal member of the Triune Godhead. Other religions have their sacred books, but there is nothing outside of Christ to compare with His and the apostles' teachings on the person and power of the Holy Spirit as revealed in the Holy Bible.

As the Administrator of the New Covenant, the Holy Spirit mediates for the believer all that is provided in Christ's birth, death, and resurrection. But the greatest tragedy of this Age of the Spirit is the widespread failure of born-again Christians to draw upon the life and power promised in a life lived in the fullness of the Holy Spirit.

A few years ago I sat in a small circle of preachers and listened as one of the evangelical movement's most admired and trusted leaders expressed his fear that most Christians in North America are living below the spiritual poverty level. He felt they are not filled with the Spirit and are therefore empty, complacent, powerless, and defeated.

The Scriptures warn us against sinning against the Holy Spirit. Jesus made it clear that how we relate to the Holy Spirit will determine the quality of our spiritual life here as well as our eternal destiny.

Our Heavenly Father and our Lord Jesus Christ have freely given us the Holy Spirit in our new birth experience. When Jesus promised this, He said of the Spirit, "He dwells with you and will be in you" (John 14:17, NKJV). Since the Holy Spirit is the Spirit of the Father and the Son, we can never really know them except by our relationship with the Holy Spirit. "Now we have received, not the spirit of the world, but the Spirit who is from God, that we might know the things that have been freely given to us by God. These things we also speak, not in words which man's wisdom teaches but which the Holy Spirit teaches, comparing spiritual things with spiritual. But the natural man does not receive the things of the Spirit of God, for they are foolishness to him; nor can he know *them*, because they are spiritually discerned" (I Corinthians 2:12-14, NKJV).

Therefore, since the Holy Spirit lives within us, we should realize that He is God and that He has come to be our Holy Guest. As our Holy Guest, He expects and deserves a holy response—love, adoration, honor, obedience, and praise. We need to remember that when we love and obey the Holy Spirit we are loving and obeying the Father and the Son.

We also need to realize that when we disobey or fail to honor the Holy Spirit, we are disobeying and dishonoring the Father and the Son. Therefore, we should be alert to the Scriptures that warn us about sinning against the Spirit—*grieving, quenching, lying to, tempting (testing),* and *presuming against the Holy Spirit.* Let's look at each one of these to better understand how serious these offenses are:

- *Grieving the Holy Spirit* (Ephesians 4:30). God fills us with His Spirit in order that we might worship Him in truth and serve Him in power. No matter how glorious our experience with God in the past, only as we live and walk in the Spirit are we enabled to live in intimate communion with Christ. Within the context of Ephesians 4:30-5:5 the apostle Paul lists some sins that grieve the Spirit: bitterness, wrath, anger, clamor, evil speaking, malice, fornication, uncleanness, covetousness, filthiness, foolish talking, coarse jesting, and idolatry. These sins, if not confessed and repented of, will rob us of the divine fullness of the Spirit. At any point where Christ is replaced from the throne of our hearts, we should immediately confess our sins and return to the fullness of the Spirit, thereby recovering from our loss. The apostle Paul argues that since Christ has "sealed" us with His Spirit, He holds every redemptive claim on us (Ephesians 1:13-14). Therefore we must learn how to live in continual reference to the Holy Spirit.

- *Quenching the Holy Spirit* (I Thessalonians 5:19, NKJV). The word "quench" means to put out, subdue, choke, suppress, stifle, or dampen. The Holy Spirit is a person who can be shut out and shut down in His work of counseling, restraining, constraining, convicting, leading, and empowering us. We are to praise and thank Him for His faithfulness. In doing so, we encourage Him to work within us to the extent that we allow Him to enable us to walk in freedom, power, and holiness.

- *Lying to the Holy Spirit* (Acts 5:2-5, NKJV). Ananias and Sapphira were both charged by the apostle Peter of lying to the Holy Spirit. Lying to the Holy Spirit is the sin of hypocrisy in which one knowingly, for whatever reason, testifies to a false devotion. The Holy Spirit had led Barnabas and other prosperous members of the early church to contribute to a fund to help the needy brothers and sisters, and Ananias and Sapphira decided to join in the program. When they sold a property, they kept back part of the proceeds. They brought a portion but claimed it to be the whole amount. Peter asked, "Ananias, why has Satan filled your heart to lie to the Holy Spirit and keep back *part* of the price of the land for yourself?" Remember, the early church body in Jerusalem was growing and casting a tremendous influence for Christ as an exemplary base for the launching of the world enterprise of spreading the Gospel. Satan attempted to use the hypocrisy of Ananias and Sapphira to corrupt the Christian movement in its infancy.

    • *Tempting (testing) the Holy Spirit* (Acts 5:7-10). After God had visited Ananias with a swift judgment of death, Sapphira came in without knowing what had happened to her husband. Peter said to her, "How is it that you have agreed together to test the Spirit of the Lord?" (Acts 5:9, NKJV); The Amplified New Testament expresses this verse: "How could you two have agreed *and* conspired together to try to deceive the Spirit of the Lord?" Tempting, or testing, the Spirit is the sin of presumption in which one seeks the sanction of the Holy Spirit on a *pretended* sacrifice of worship. It is sad to realize that the first recorded sin in the life of the early church was the love of praise for a pretended sacrifice in giving.

    The apostle Peter had reminded Ananias that he and his wife "have not lied to men but to God" (v. 4). The dire consequences of sudden death for both was not a decision or an act of the apostles or the deacons of the Jerusalem Church but a swift judgment by God Himself. God could not allow the members of that church body to become corrupted by those who attempted to seek divine sanction on their false worship.

    God's act of immediate judgment had a tremendously purifying effect: "great fear came upon all the church and upon all who heard these things" (v. 11, NKJV). The verses following revealed heart-searching for half-heartedness, pretense, and any kind or form of hypocrisy. There was a mighty revival as a result of God's judgment which introduced humility, heart-searching, repentance, and renewal: ". . . through the hands of the apostles many signs and wonders were done among the people" (v. 12). "And believers were increasingly added to the Lord, multitudes of both men and women, so that they brought the sick out into the streets and laid *them* on beds and couches, that at least the shadow of Peter passing by might fall on some of them. Also a multitude gathered from the surrounding cities to Jerusalem, bringing sick people and those who were tormented by unclean spirits, and they were all healed" (vv. 14-16).

    • *Presuming against the Holy Spirit.* (This deserves extra attention and will be explained in the next chapter.)

Prayer: Lord, thank You for Your indwelling Holy Spirit who is given us to know You, enjoy You, love You, and obey You. Your presence is a constant reminder that the power You bring is not because of correct doctrine but because the Holy Spirit enables us to believe and behave as Your Word commands.

How I praise You that Your Spirit convicts me of thoughts and attitudes that would lead to sinning against His holy will for my life. And even when I have weakened and actually grieved or quenched the Spirit, His convicting presence has made it possible for me to repent and receive forgiveness and restoration to the Spirit-led life.

Lord, keep me sensitive to Your Spirit so that I can continue to walk in fellowship with an ungrieved Holy Spirit. Amen!

16

The Sin of Presuming Against the Spirit

"Of how much worse punishment, do you suppose, will he be thought worthy who has trampled the Son of God underfoot, counted the blood of the covenant by which he was sanctified a common thing, and insulted the Spirit of grace?" (Hebrews 10:29, NKJV)

Nearly all the surveys on the state of the American church show that most are in agreement that the North American church is in desperate need of a mighty spiritual awakening. The smell of spiritual death is so strong in many church services until even some of the traditional and nominal members are repulsed. In such an atmosphere where the presence of the Holy Spirit is not even recognized, gifted performers can create an amazing human glory which can be easily mistaken for divine reality. But no dressed up and pumped up artificial life-signs can take the place of the Spirit of Life.

We desperately need the wind and fire of Pentecost. But it is time to face the truth: *no great revival can come to America until Christians repent of their presumption and regain a New Testament sensitivity to the Holy Spirit.*

Please understand, in referring to *the sin of presuming against the Holy Spirit,* I am not referring to the sin of "blasphemy against the Spirit" (Matthew 12:31) or "the Unpardonable Sin." No, I'm referring to the sin against the Holy Spirit that is committed so freely by many who have been born again and in whom the Holy Spirit abides. I am speaking of those who have the Holy Spirit, but who are living selfishly, disobediently, worldly, and carelessly—some of whom are claiming that it makes no difference at all.

Let's consider the meaning of the word *presume*. Generally, it means to assume, to suppose, or to take for granted. But it also means to take advantage of a truth or a fact and to stretch it beyond its context. Further, to presume means to venture beyond due authority and to proceed with unwarranted or inappropriate boldness without proper consultation or respect, and to take liberties without official consent. Presumption can progress to the dangerous point of pretending sanction from above for a very self-exalting action!

I fear that the sin of presuming against the Holy Spirit is more common among evangelicals than we realize. Claiming to be filled with the Spirit while going on in selfish, fleshly, carnal living is grieving to our Holy Guest. But, God be praised, it is not unpardonable; there is forgiveness for us! Our assurance is, "If we confess our sins, He is faithful and just to forgive us our sins and to cleanse us from all unrighteousness" (I John 1:9, NKJV).

I meet some presumptive arguments from professing Christians who claim that once they were "by one Spirit baptized into one body" they need not pray for the fullness of the Spirit. My response is, "Come on, please look more closely and honestly at this passage—let's finish the verse"—"and have all been made to drink into one Spirit" (I Corinthians 12:13, NKJV). Yes, in the new birth we were christened by the Spirit, constituted a true member of the body of Christ by the Spirit. In that moment of believing we became indwelt by the gift of the Holy Spirit. But for what purpose?—"to drink"! Note the *New English Bible* (*NEB)* translation of this: "one Holy Spirit was poured out for all of us to drink." But we must keep on drinking—we must keep on being "filled with the Spirit" (Ephesians 5:18). The filling of the Spirit is not a once-for-all experience. The idea of the followers of Christ being renewed in the Spirit by being refilled is taught by our Lord: "If anyone thirsts, let him come to Me and drink. He who believes in Me, as the Scripture has said, out of his heart will flow rivers of living water." But this He spoke concerning the Spirit, whom those believing in Him would receive; for the Holy Spirit was not yet *given*, because Jesus was not yet glorified" (John 7:37-39, NKJV).

The Holy Spirit has been given to believers in order that we might continue to thirst for Him. God entrusts to us as His born-again children a thirst for more of His Son, Jesus Christ. We are commanded by the apostle Peter to "grow in the grace and knowledge of our Lord and Savior Jesus Christ" (II Peter 3:18, NKJV). The believer who is never renewed in the Spirit has stopped growing spiritually.

Jesus warned His disciples against taking the Holy Spirit for granted. Throughout His three years of training them, He placed more emphasis on their receiving and relating to the Holy Spirit than on any other subject. He told them to "stay in the city until you have been clothed with power from on high" (Luke 24:49).

The wisest thing the apostles and early believers ever did was to obey the Lord and pray and wait for the coming of the Holy Spirit. The wisest thing modern Christians can do today is return to the Upper Room to pray for a renewing of the Spirit. Let us remember that God gives the Holy Spirit only to those believers who hunger, ask, believe, and obey. Jesus said, "If you then, being evil, know how to give good gifts to your children, how much more will *your* heavenly Father give the Holy Spirit to those who ask Him" (Luke 11:13, NKJV).

Jesus made it clear that God will not entrust the Holy Spirit to a prayerless believer, nor will He pour out His Spirit on a prayerless church. Actually, our prayerlessness grieves the Holy Spirit. It robs us of the presence of God and the Spirit's demonstrations of power in our worship services. When we are weak in prayer, we experience little conviction of sin, few people find Christ, and there is little passion among church members for holiness of heart and life.

The North American church is being mercifully given time in which to repent of prayerlessness and presumption against the Holy Spirit. We must pray and believe God to give a sweeping tidal wave of His presence on His people all over our nation. This can only come as we meet the divine conditions set forth in His Holy Word:

> "If my people, who are called by my name, will humble themselves and pray and seek my face and turn from their wicked ways, then will I hear from heaven and will forgive their sin and will heal their land" (II Chronicles 7:14).

Only then will God send a revival to individuals, churches, and nations.

- Revival alone will bring Pentecostal purity and power back to the church.
- Revival comes as the wind of the Spirit breathes new life into the lukewarmness and deadness of God's people.
- Revival is the water of the Spirit breaking forth on dry souls in abundance—downpouring, infilling, outflowing.
- Revival is the oil of the Spirit flowing forth to heal our diseased hearts and broken lives, refill our flickering lamps, and anoint our weak souls.
- Revival is the dove of the Spirit descending with peace and purity upon our anguished spirits and divided hearts.
- Revival is the mantle of the Spirit falling on the church to clothe her with Christ's power for living and loving and witnessing to a needy world.

Revival power is altar power, so it's time to repair our broken altars, gather in our upper rooms, and confess our sins against the Holy Spirit. In response to such humility and repentance, our faithful God will roar from His Holy Mountain and revive His people once again.

Prayer: Lord, I ask Your forgiveness for my slowness in discerning the stirrings of Your Spirit in my heart and life. I now pray for a greater degree of sensitivity to Your Spirit that will help me detect early the source of my thoughts and the nature of my considered actions. Like our Lord Jesus while on earth, I long to sense the purpose of the Father for each day and receive from the Spirit the wisdom and power to carry out His will.

May I remember early in each day to ask the Spirit to clear my mind, cleanse my heart, and condition my inner person to think in the Spirit, pray in the Spirit, and walk in the Spirit. Above all, please help me to so live in the Spirit that I never commit the sin of presuming against the Holy Spirit. Amen!

17

The Spirit of Intercession

"Then he said to them, 'Suppose one of you has a friend, and he goes to him at midnight and says, "Friend, lend me three loaves of bread, because a friend of mine on a journey has come to me, and I have nothing to set before him."

"Then the one inside answers, 'Don't bother me. The door is already locked, and my children are with me in bed. I can't get up and give you anything.' I tell you, though he will not get up and give him the bread because he is his friend, yet because of the man's boldness he will get up and give him as much as he needs.

"So I say to you: Ask and it will be given to you; seek and you will find; knock and the door will be opened to you. For everyone who asks receives; he who seeks finds; and to him who knocks, the door will be opened.

"Which of you fathers, if your son asks for a fish, will give him a snake instead? Or if he asks for an egg, will give him a scorpion? If you then, though you are evil, know how to give good gifts to your children, how much more will your Father in heaven give the Holy Spirit to those who ask him" (Luke 11:5-13).

Jesus taught His disciples that the kingdom of God moves forward by intercessory prayer. Those who would lead their loved ones and neighbors to Christ must learn the secrets of intercession. Life in the Spirit comes with a passion to reach the lost around the world, those within our families, and the neighbors next door.

Jesus gave a powerful illustration on how intercession works. We could call it the parable of "The Intercession Triangle." One person turns to another person on behalf of still a third person. Note the three parties of the triangle: a compassionate friend, a hungry and weary traveler, and a resourceful person.

But let's be fair to the story—it's a parable, not an allegory. In a parable only one fundamental truth is presented; the details are incidental. In this parable, the major point is the need for bold, persistent asking; but the fundamental truth in this story does not have to do with the nature of God. Jesus is not teaching that God is in bed fast asleep and refuses to be bothered about the needs of His children. No, Jesus is not comparing the Father to the sleeping friend. In fact, He is contrasting the two. He's arguing from the lesser to the greater. In other words, the more hesitant the sleeping friend is to comply with the request, the more willing our Heavenly Father is to grant us all we ask for.

Christian believers everywhere need to see the key principle in seeking to pray for unsaved friends and loved ones and to intercede for revival in the church—or for anything they believe to be the will of God. But let us not forget that the last verse in this parable makes it clear that the intercessor's greatest need is that of the *much-moreness,* or *abundance,* or *fullness* of the Holy Spirit.

True intercessory prayer begins at the point of discovering our innate weakness and surrendering our mind and will to the Holy Spirit in return for His fullness. In this we are exchanging our weakness for His power and our emptiness for His fullness.

All around us—in our own homes, in our neighborhoods, at distances beyond our city or state—are loved ones and acquaintances who need Jesus Christ as Savior. God loves each and every one of them, but He has ordained to work in cooperation with His earthly witnesses to draw them to His Son in saving grace. For He does not want them to be lost. And He has called each one of us, His redeemed ones, saying, "When the Holy Spirit comes on you . . . you will be my witnesses" (Acts 1:8).

A Spirit-inspired intercessor makes an ideal Spirit-inspired witness. God has not called us to witness to everyone but to witness to those who are within our sphere of influence. When the Spirit lays someone on my heart, I take it as a sign that I am to begin praying for that person or that family. After a time, I'll realize I'm to follow up on my praying with a heart-to-heart conversation, led by the Spirit. Realizing that I must earn the right to testify to those I'm concerned about, I ask a few questions about their personal spiritual standing with the Lord. Afterward, I can usually discern if they know Christ as Savior; if they appear not to know, I give a personal testimony. But all the time I'm depending on the Holy Spirit to prepare their heart for the salvation the Lord wants to give them.

As a witness for Christ, I know that I am not persuasive enough to convince unbelievers that they need to trust in Jesus as their Savior. I am dependent on the Holy Spirit to bring them to a deep hunger and prepare them for repentance and faith. The Holy Trinity—the Father, the Son, and the Holy Spirit—are ready, willing, and delighted to bring the ones I've been interceding for to the new birth by the Holy Spirit. Almighty God is our Resource for effective witnessing.

As intercessors, let's keep in mind that we are not left to ourselves. We have access to the leadership of the Holy Spirit as to whom we are to witness—even the circumstances under which we are to meet. The Spirit will direct us on how to personally testify, what questions we are to ask, and when we are to ask the question—"Are you ready now to confess Jesus Christ as your Savior and ask His forgiveness for sin and live for Him with His help?"

Good intercessors always follow up with much prayer for the persons they lead to the Lord. They look to the Spirit for guidance on how to pray for them and what literature to give them. They invite them to worship with them or, if this is not feasible, they recommend another Bible-believing church or group.

Every soul-winner needs to remember that leading someone to Christ carries with it the responsibility of discipleship. As someone has observed, "Disciples are made, not born." Once one is born again, he or she must be discipled. Jesus commanded, "Go and *make* disciples." Those led to Christ must be made aware of the Holy Spirit who has come to live within them. We must give them an understanding about how to follow the leadership of the indwelling Spirit. This is a vital part of the discipleship process.

The weary traveler in our parable arrived at midnight, an inconvenient hour for both the compassionate friend and the resourceful party. But Spirit-filled intercessors must rely on the Holy Spirit for the determination, faith, and commitment to follow through until the ones they pray for and pray with are touched by the Holy Spirit and have an opportunity to either receive or reject the Lord Jesus Christ as Savior and Lord.

All true disciples of our Lord Jesus Christ are commanded to witness for Christ and to make disciples of those who come to know the Lord. This means prayer, energy, and times of connecting with new believers when it is not always convenient. There may be disappointments, but we must be faithful. Of all our "works of righteousness" for which we shall be rewarded, I believe winning the lost and making disciples of those we win should be our prime commitment. None of us should stand before the Judgment Seat of Christ without having won others to our Lord!

Prayer: Lord Jesus, I thank You for those—my dear mother, Estelle, and the evangelists Joe Youmans, John Newby, and Woody Shields, who lovingly told me what Jesus Christ meant to them and how He had changed their lives and led them into a life of wise decisions and inward peace. And I'm glad they took the time to point out to me that God so loved me that He sacrificed His one and only Son to pay for my sins with His death on the cross—that "without the shedding of blood there is no forgiveness" (Hebrews 9:22).

Lord, I'm asking Your Holy Spirit to impart to me Your passion for the lost, that I will love them, long for their salvation, weep over their lostness, and beg them to have "an ear to hear" the Spirit's call to repentance and eternal life.

Give me courage, freedom, and expressions that will gain and hold their interest until I realize Your Spirit is at work convicting them. Then, help me to close the presentation in such a manner that they'll know they aren't being pressured by me to make this important decision; they'll realize they are being drawn by the Holy Spirit to become a born-again child of God.

Lord, give me a glorious appreciation of the Gospel of Jesus Christ, which is "the power of God for the salvation of everyone who believes" (Romans 1:16). Holy Spirit, enable me to be faithful in intercessory prayer for the lost. Amen!

18

The Spirit of Anointing

"The scroll of the prophet Isaiah was handed to him. Unrolling it, he found the place where it is written: 'The Spirit of the Lord is on me, because he has anointed me to preach good news to the poor. He has sent me to proclaim freedom for the prisoners and recovery of sight for the blind, to release the oppressed, to proclaim the year of the Lord's favor'" (Luke 4:17-19).

"But you have an anointing from the Holy One, and all of you know the truth" (I John 2:20).

In the Book of Exodus we read of the Lord telling Moses to develop an anointing oil for the purpose of anointing Aaron and his sons to serve Him as priests of the tabernacle. This "sacred anointing oil" was of such a rare quality that it was to be made of the fragrant blend of the best olive oil and rare spices. Anyone caught duplicating and marketing this sacred oil was to be "cut off from his people" (Exodus 30:22-33).
   In Old Testament times prophets were called to anoint men for three offices: prophets, priests, and kings. This sacred anointing oil was usually applied to the head (probably the forehead) of one called of God to be set apart for one or more of these particular offices.

Whether during the period of the Law or in these New Testament times of grace, the idea of anointing is that of setting apart a person for a divine purpose. Jesus Christ was the "Anointed One" (Acts 4:26). Any Christian believer is a Christ-one—someone who has been anointed by the same Spirit who anointed Christ. The apostle Paul reminded the believers in Ephesus: "Having believed, you were marked in him [Christ] with a seal, the promised Holy Spirit, who is a deposit guaranteeing our inheritance until the redemption of those who are God's possession—to the praise of his glory" (Ephesians 1:13-14).

Prophets were anointed and set apart for delivering God's messages to His people and to the world. They were also to live as witnesses and examples of His message.

Priests were anointed to stand before God and pray intercessory prayers for His people. Our Lord shares His priestly ministry with all who follow Him and who will receive the anointing of His Spirit. The apostle Peter would remind us that we "are being built into a spiritual house to be a holy priesthood, offering spiritual sacrifices acceptable to God through Jesus Christ" (I Peter 2:5). And Peter continued, "But you are a chosen people, a royal priesthood, a holy nation, a people belonging to God, that you may declare the praises of him who called you out of darkness into his wonderful light" (I Peter 2:9).

Kings were anointed to govern and rule according to the will and Word of the Sovereign Almighty to whom all nations and individuals are accountable, including the kings themselves.

The Holy Spirit is given at our new birth in regeneration. This is meant to be the beginning of our relationship with the Holy Spirit in which we are to experience all that Jesus promised in the *Paraclete* passages of the Gospel of John (chapters 14 through 16). Unless we develop an "ear to hear what the Spirit says to the churches [to the believers]" (Revelation 2:4), we will never know His convicting, comforting, counseling, and cleansing. Unless we are "filled with the Spirit" (Ephesians 5:18) and keep on being filled with the Spirit, we'll fall into the tragic condition of "having a form of godliness but denying its power" (II Timothy 3:5).

We must learn how to relate to the Holy Spirit. He is a Person who thinks, feels, speaks, listens, wills, and acts. He makes our Heavenly Father and our Lord Jesus Christ real to us. He is our access to our Great High Priest, our Savior, to whom we approach at the "throne of grace" for our needs of mercy and grace (Hebrews 4:14-16).

How wonderful that God's plan of salvation is to include His very Spirit to indwell us! The apostle Paul writes in I Corinthians 3:16, "Don't you know that you yourselves are God's temple and that God's Spirit lives in you?" Since we are privileged to host Him, our Holy Guest, should we not pay attention to what He likes, what He needs, what He stands for, what His purpose is? May the Lord help each of us to develop a deep sensitivity to the Holy Spirit within us!

Without the Holy Spirit—

- we cannot live the Christian life. He is our Counselor (Helper) (John 14:16).

- we will not have the truth; He is "the Spirit of truth" (John 14:17).

- we will not learn what the Scriptures teach (John 14:26).

- we can never know the full truth about Jesus (John 16:15).

- we will not know what to pray for (John 16:23).

- we will never know the fullness of joy (John 16:22).

- we cannot have power to worship, witness, or work for our Lord (Acts 1:8; John 4:24).

- we cannot walk in holiness and power (I Thessalonians 4:7-8).

The Christian life was planned by our Heavenly Father to be a life anointed by the Spirit from the time of our new birth to the time of our death or Rapture. The apostle Paul wrote of "the law of the Spirit" liberating us "from the law of sin and death" (Romans 8:2). And then he explained, "For those who live according to the flesh set their minds on the things of the flesh, but those who living according to the Spirit, the things of the Spirit. For to be carnally minded is death, but to be spiritually minded is life and peace" (Romans 8:5-6). This antithesis between *flesh* and *Spirit* is dominant in Paul's epistle to the Romans and is continued in Corinthians, Galatians, Ephesians, Philippians, Colossians, and I Timothy. The apostle's emphasis is that the Spirit's anointing, if not violated or ignored, liberates the believer from bondage to the *flesh*. We are not left to our own human mental and volitional strengths for living the Christian life. We are enabled by the Spirit to produce "the fruit of the Spirit—love, joy, peace, longsuffering, kindness, goodness, faithfulness, gentleness, and self-control" (Galatians 5:22-23, NKJV). This is the Christ-like life we have been predestined for—"in Him also we have obtained an inheritance, being predestined according to the purpose of Him who works all things according to the counsel of His will" (Ephesians 1:11, NKJV). Again, Paul writes the Corinthians, "Now the Lord is the Spirit; and where the Spirit of the Lord *is*, there *is* liberty. But we all, with unveiled face, beholding as in a mirror the glory of the Lord, are being transformed into the same image from glory to glory, just as by the Spirit of the Lord" (II Corinthians 3:17-18, NKJV).

The apostle Paul is faithful to remind believers that the secret of our spiritual success is the anointing of the Holy Spirit. Therefore he urges, "Walk in the Spirit, and you shall not fulfill the lust of the flesh. For the flesh lusts against the Spirit, and the Spirit against the flesh; and these are contrary to one another, so that you do not do the things that you wish. But if you are led by the Spirit, you are not under the law" (Galatians 5:16-18, NKJV).

Prayer: O Spirit of the living God and Spirit of our Lord Jesus Christ, thank You for drawing me to You to confess You as my Savior and Lord, for indwelling me from the moment of my new birth, for marking me with the seal of Your possession, and for adopting me into Your family of the redeemed. You have remained faithful throughout my life to keep me in Your love and to help me understand Your Word. You have strengthened me when I've been weak and renewed and restored me when I've realized and confessed my faltering and failing. How thankful I am for Your anointing!

Now, Lord, help me to remain sensitive to Your Holy Spirit and walk in the joy and power of fellowship with You. I would know the fullness of the Spirit—the fullness of His love, the fullness of His joy, the fullness of His peace, the fullness of His power, and the fullness of His plan for my life.

Oh, God, I feel the need to ask that You expand my capacity for sensing Your presence, comprehending Your majestic holiness, and appreciating Your awesome glory. I truly long to be consumed by Your transcendent Being. Please grant it, Lord Jesus! Amen!

19

The Spirit of the Throne and the Altar

"In the year that King Uzziah died, I saw the Lord seated on a throne, high and exalted, and the train of his robe filled the temple. Above him were seraphs, each with six wings: With two wings they covered their faces, with two they covered their feet, and with two they were flying. And they were calling to one another: 'Holy, holy, holy is the Lord Almighty; the whole earth is full of his glory.'

"At the sound of their voices the doorposts and thresholds shook and the temple was filled with smoke.

"'Woe to me!' I cried. 'I am ruined! For I am a man of unclean lips, and I live among a people of unclean lips, and my eyes have seen the King, the Lord Almighty.'

"Then one of the seraphs flew to me with a live coal in his hand, which he had taken with tongs from the altar. With it he touched my mouth and said, 'See, this has touched your lips; your guilt is taken away and your sin atoned for!'

"Then I heard the voice of the Lord saying, 'Whom shall I send? And who will go for us?'

"And I said, 'Here am I. Send me!'

"He said, 'Go and tell this people: Be ever hearing, but never understanding; be ever seeing, but never perceiving'" (Isaiah 6:1-9).

The name of the prophet Isaiah means "God saves." There are two very significant objects—the throne and the altar—that are instrumental in accomplishing the salvation of the prophet and reveal God's plan of redemption for all of Adam's fallen race. Therefore, let us consider in the prophet's vision two glorious truths: the glory of the throne and the grace from the altar.

The Glory of the Throne

Isaiah declares, "I saw the Lord seated on a throne, high and exalted, and the train of his robe filled the temple." The prophet had been familiar with the regal pomp and royal circumstances of King Uzziah's administration. But the king is dead, and the prophet had never seen anything in the kingly courts or the temple of worship to compare with this vision that was about to transform his inner being and redirect the rest of his life.

Isaiah saw a solemn and soul-searching vision of the Lord Jesus Christ "seated on a throne." Yes, the prophet saw the very one and only Son whom God would "raise from the dead and seat . . . at his right hand in the heavenly realms, far above all authority, power and dominion, and every title that can be given" (Ephesians 1:20-21). The prophet's reaction to such a manifestation of glory was about the same as that of the Israelites after seeing the God of glory opening the Red Sea for them: "Who is like you—majestic in holiness, awesome in glory, working wonders" (Exodus 15:11).

The Spirit of God caused Isaiah to see what John would later see in Jesus Christ—"We have seen his glory, the glory of the One and Only, who came from the Father, full of grace and truth" (John 1:14). "The true light that gives light to every man" (John 1:9). Something about the glory of Jesus Christ caused Isaiah to realize his spiritual and moral darkness. He had been gazing upon the One whom God sent into the world to become the perfect standard by which every moral being must be measured before the Almighty Judge. Perhaps for the first time, Isaiah realized it was not what he thought of himself, nor was it important what others thought of him; he had for the first time seen the truth about his true inner being—"Woe to me! . . . I am ruined! For I am a man of unclean lips, and I live among a people of unclean lips, and my eyes have seen the King, the Lord Almighty." The light that shone from the throne convicted the prophet of his sinful condition and prepared him for his confession of sin, which made him ready for the redemption that awaited him.

The Grace from the Altar

Isaiah's vision was solemnizing and convincing. Never before had the inner chambers of his heart been exposed. Who and what he was became known to him. It was confession time: "I am ruined"—*undone, unrighteous, unfit, unprepared*! Christ's moral glory so poured out on the prophet's soul until he had no excuse, no plea, and no defense. He was sinfully lost and at the mercy of the One so gloriously revealed.

Following Isaiah's confession, his attention was called to the activity around the *altar*—"then one of the seraphs flew to me with a live coal in his hand, which he had taken with tongs from the altar. With it he touched my mouth and said, 'See, this has touched your lips; your guilt is taken away and your sin atoned for!'"

God's provisions for man's lostness is not only ample; it is extravagant. The guilt of sin revealed by the vision was removed by grace from the altar, his sin had been paid for, and by believing his guilt was gone.

Isaiah's vision is a clear and convicting message of the Gospel of Jesus Christ: "For God so loved the world that he gave his one and only Son, that whoever believes in him shall not perish but have eternal life. For God did not send his Son into the world to condemn the world, but to save the world through him. Whoever believes in him is not condemned, but whoever does not believe stands condemned already because he has not believed in the name of God's one and only Son" (John 3:16-18).

In Isaiah's experience we can see the *ruin* of sinful man and then the complete *redemption* through Jesus Christ. The Holy Spirit has been sent from Heaven to earth to prepare our minds and hearts for salvation: "When he comes, he will convict the world of guilt in regard to sin and righteousness and judgment" (John 16:8). Our response of faith and surrender to His conviction will bring the miracle of the new birth. Jesus told Nicodemus, "no one can see the kingdom of God unless he is born again" (John 3:3). According to Jesus, the new birth comes by a miracle of the Holy Spirit (John 3:8).

Our moment of salvation may not come like the glorious vision of Isaiah. But each of us must respond seriously to the Holy Spirit's convicting us of sin and leading us to believe in our Lord Jesus Christ's atoning death on Calvary's cross as full payment for our sins. We must believe in Christ as the Son of God and call upon Him and personally make our confession of faith. We are assured, "That if you confess with your mouth, 'Jesus is Lord,' and believe in your heart that God raised him from the dead, you will be saved. For it is with your heart that you believe and are justified, and it is with your mouth that you confess and are saved" (Romans 10:9-10). What amazing grace!

The Holy Spirit is faithful to convict us of sin; as we repent, confess, and believe, He is faithful to apply the atoning blood of Christ to our hearts and assure us of eternal life. He also takes up residence within us, sealing us as children of God. Having been born of the Spirit we are commanded to "worship in Spirit" (John 4:24), "pray in the Spirit" (Ephesians 6:18; Jude 20), "live by the Spirit" (Galatians 5:16), and "be filled with the Spirit" (Ephesians 5:18), meaning "keep on being filled with the Spirit" in times of spiritual renewal.

Prayer: Lord Jesus, remembering that You said, "Blessed are those who hunger and thirst for righteousness, for they will be filled" (Matthew 5:6), I need to ask You to help me with my hunger for the cleansing You give. May I be broken and penitent over my selfishness, worldliness, and carelessness. Help me long for Your purifying power in my heart and life. I thank You for being faithful to convict me and help me with my repentance. But, Lord, I am determined by Your grace to reach a place of stability in my relationship with You so that I receive Your enablement to resist temptation and live in victory over sin. Help me stay full of Your Holy Spirit and walk in the influence of Your constant Presence.

Thank You for the Spirit of the Throne and the Altar. Amen!

20

The Spirit of Blessing

"Jabez cried out to the God of Israel, 'Oh, that you would bless me and enlarge my territory! Let your hand be with me, and keep me from harm so that I will be free from pain.' And God granted his request" (I Chronicles 4:10).

"And afterward, I will pour out my Spirit on all people. Your sons and daughters will prophesy, your old men will dream dreams, your young men will see visions. Even on my servants, both men and women, I will pour out my Spirit in those days" (Joel 2:28-29).

"But you will receive power when the Holy Spirit comes on you; and you will be my witnesses in Jerusalem, and in all Judea and Samaria, and to the ends of the earth" (Acts 1:8).

"If you then, though you are evil, know how to give good gifts to your children, how much more will your Father in heaven give the Holy Spirit to those who ask him" (Luke 11:13).

The words "bless" and "blessing" are used over a thousand times in the Old and New Testaments. The first appearance is when God blessed the creatures of the sea and the birds of the air and ordered them to "be fruitful and increase in number" (Genesis 1:22).

Finally, "God created man in his own image . . . male and female he created them" (Genesis 1:27). And then the Word declares that "God blessed them" (Genesis 1:28) and ordered them to be fruitful and rule over the fish of the sea, the birds of the air, and over every living creature that moves on the ground.

God's blessing on Noah was the secret of his escape from the flood. He and his family were blessed by being delivered from judgment, and they were blessed by divine provisions after the flood.

But let us consider the most gracious blessing God ever gave the human race: "For God so loved the world that he gave his one and only Son, that whoever believes in him shall not perish but have eternal life. For God did not send his Son into the world to condemn the world, but to save the world through him. Whoever believes in him is not condemned, but whoever does not believe stands condemned already because he has not believed in the name of God's one and only Son" (John 3:16-18).

I shall never forget the moment I knelt in prayer and believed in God's one and only Son! I knew instantly that my sins had been forgiven, I had found peace with God, and I was entering into eternal life. The blessing that came with my salvation could never be compared with any other blessing in my whole life.

But let's remember that Jesus promised His followers an amazing blessing in sending the Holy Spirit to empower them for living the Christian life: "But the Counselor, the Holy Spirit, whom the Father will send in my name, will teach you all things and will remind you of everything I have said to you" (John 14:26); "When the Counselor comes, whom I will send to you from the Father, the Spirit of truth who goes out from the Father, he will testify about me" (John 15:26); "But I tell you the truth: It is for your good that I am going away. Unless I go away, the Counselor will not come to you; but if I go, I will send him to you. When he comes, he will convict the world of guilt in regard to sin and righteousness and judgment: in regard to sin, because men do not believe in me; in regard to righteousness, because I am going to the Father, where you can see me no longer; and in regard to judgment, because the prince of this world now stands condemned" (John 16:7-11).

The salvation blessings of the born-again, Spirit-indwelt believer cannot be compared with any earthly blessing that comes to a mortal being. Jesus asked, "What good is it for a man to gain the whole world, yet forfeit his soul? Or what can a man give in exchange for his soul? If anyone is ashamed of me and my words in this adulterous and sinful generation, the Son of Man will be ashamed of him when he comes in his Father's glory with the holy angels" (Mark 8:36-38).

How it must grieve the Father, the Son, and the Holy Spirit that multitudes are seeking all kinds of blessings during their earthly journey, while neglecting the blessing of eternal life and all the other many blessings God has in store for His redeemed children!

Once in a while I meet a believer who gets deep into the Word of God and catches on to what God promises persons who will believe with their total being what they are reading and decide to go all out on those promises.

Let's consider an Old Testament character—his name is Jabez. "Jabez cried out to the God of Israel, 'Oh, that you would bless me and enlarge my territory! Let your hand be with me, and keep me from harm so that I will be free from pain.' And God granted his request" (I Chronicles 4:10). Most Old Testament Bible scholars believe that Ezra authored this book and that it was his purpose to try and restore Israel's confidence and obedience as a people of God. As we read the prayer of Jabez we come to realize it was no mere mental piece of poetry—it was the deep cry of a soul that could not stand the thought of living without the anointing and favor of one so good, glorious, and all-powerful as the God who promises to bless His people! Consider the same prayer from another translation: "Jabez prayed to the God of Israel: 'Bless me, O bless me! Give me land, large tracts of land. And provide your personal protection—don't let evil hurt me.' God gave him what he asked" (I Chronicles 4:10, The Message).

As you are reading this message today, you could be feeling that there ought to be more to your Christian faith than you've realized up to now. Could it be that the Spirit of God is calling you to a new level of praying the will of God in your thinking, in your relationships, and in your worship of God? Believe me, our gracious God is looking for believers who are hungry to discover His power, follow his commands, and reach out to some lost and confused people in this messed up world.

Would you be willing to pray a passionate, desperate prayer like that of Jabez and have it reach the ears of an Almighty God who can fill you with His Spirit? The Holy Spirit is the Spirit of *holiness,* the Spirit of *power*, the Spirit of *wisdom*, the Spirit of *love*—and even the Spirit of *a holy boldness* in prayer, obedience, and faith!

Consider another Old Testament character who prayed a sincere and desperate prayer that changed the course of his life. After he had wrestled in prayer all night with God, Jacob grabbed hold of the Lord's angel and said, "I will not let you go unless you bless me" (Genesis 32:26). Then, it is recorded that "he blessed him there" (Genesis 32:29).

Prayer: Please, God, give Your praying people in our nation a sense of how we must humble ourselves and pray and seek Your face in this critical hour! We appear to be straying from our spiritual foundations, and we need to repent and return to You. Would You raise up Spirit-anointed men, such as Jacob and Jabez, who will sense our times and plead for Your merciful intervention in every area of our society? Cause their burdened hearts to cry out to You for the parents in our homes, the preachers in our churches, the politicians in our governments, and the professors in our universities.

Lord, would You also raise up godly women like Hannah and Anna—women who gave themselves to the kind of praying that changed the course of a nation and the world? Hannah's grief over the backsliding of Israel prompted her to call on the Lord for a child which she would dedicate to the Lord to turn the people back to God. "In bitterness of soul Hannah wept much and prayed to the Lord. And she made a vow, saying, 'O Lord Almighty, if you will only look upon your servant's misery and remember me, and not forget your servant but give her a son, then I will give him to the Lord for all the days of his life' . . ." (I Samuel 1:10-11). God heard her cry and gave her a son, Samuel, whose prophetic and priestly ministries helped to restore righteousness and order.

We also read about Anna the prophetess who blessed and gave thanks for Baby Jesus. "She was very old; she had lived with her husband seven years after her marriage and then was a widow until she was eighty-four. She never left the temple but worshiped night and day, fasting and praying. Coming up to them [Joseph, Mary, and Baby

Jesus] at that very moment, she gave thanks to God and spoke about the child to all who were looking forward to the redemption of Jerusalem" (Luke 2:36-38).

Who else but God can save America? God Himself has told us the way out of our moral, spiritual, social, and economic dilemma. He promised, "If my people, who are called by my name, will humble themselves and pray and seek my face and turn from their wicked ways, then I will hear from heaven and will forgive their sin and will heal their land" (II Chronicles 7:14).

Our Heavenly Father, I want to be one of Your many redeemed children who will seek Your blessing in order to pray in faith for another historic spiritual awakening in our nation. Let us pray as Jesus did: "During the days of Jesus' life on earth, he offered up prayers and petitions with loud cries and tears . . . and he was heard because of his reverent submission" (Hebrews 5:7).

Lord, teach us to pray in faith, with passion, and with pure hearts! Amen!

21

The Spirit of Burning Hearts

"Then their eyes were opened and they recognized him, and he disappeared from their sight. They asked each other, 'Were not our hearts burning within us while he talked with us on the road and opened the Scriptures to us?'" (Luke 24:31-32).

"I have come to bring fire on the earth, and how I wish it were already kindled!" (Luke 12:49).

"For this reason I remind you to fan into flame the gift of God, which is in you through the laying on of my hands. For God did not give us a spirit of timidity, but a spirit of power, of love and of self-discipline" (II Timothy 1:6-7).

The strange cycle of the backsliding and renewing of the people of God across the centuries is a haunting phenomenon. The Old Testament children of Israel often failed to meet the conditions of their covenant with Jehovah, and the resulting apostasy wrote tragedy into their history. New Testament Christian believers are just as guilty of grieving the Holy Spirit who lives within them. Sin in the lives of Christians is not without serious consequences. Our Lord Jesus Christ warned that we do not remain spiritually alive unconditionally; we experience abundant life only as we abide in Christ. He warned of withering and dying spiritually (John 15:5-8).

Five of the seven churches addressed by our Lord in chapters 1 and 2 of Revelation were commanded to repent! That same call is going out to the slumbering body of Christ in these early decades of the twenty-first century. If pastors and Christian leaders realized what is about to come to pass in America and on the face of the whole earth, they would be calling for solemn assemblies—meetings of fasting, praying, pleading for divine mercies: forgiveness, cleansing, renewed faith, deliverance from evil bondages, salvaged homes, and restoration of peace in communities.

The late Peter Marshall once wrote, "We can wear out on our knees praying for revival, but if we are not willing to go through the pain of repentance, the Great Awakening we seek will not come." (*From Sea to Shining Sea,* Fleming H. Revell, publisher, 1986, p. 406).

A good question for professing believers to ask themselves would be: What have I been doing in relation with the Holy Spirit who indwells me? Am I being obedient? Am I grieving Him? Am I quenching Him? Am I ignoring Him? If so, then we need what the apostle Paul prescribed for his spiritual son Timothy—we need to allow the Holy Spirit to rekindle His fire within us! The fire of the Holy Spirit is not wild, weird, or hyped emotions on our part. It is holy fire, purifying fire, and anointing fire! It cleanses us from the sins of fear, lust, greed, pride, and worldliness. Holy fire dispels darkness, reveals the truth, removes strongholds, and liberates from bondage.

So many of our American believers are like Cleopas and his fellow doubting disciple whom Jesus found on the Emmaus road—full of gloom and doom, taken over by doubt and dread, and full of negativism and cynicism. All of this on Resurrection Day!

But the Risen One had come alongside them; before He left them, they had recovered from their darkness and were rejoicing over burning hearts! Satan is out to try and keep us in this ugly spiritual smog so that we fail to see Jesus in His power and glory and beauty. Let's repent of our unbelief, believe God to send the fire, turn on the lights, and help us walk in the freedom and fullness of the Holy Spirit!

Are you hungry for a fresh visitation of the Holy Spirit? It will change your heart from resentment to rejoicing, from doubt to delight, from being downcast to dancing. A fresh anointing of the Holy Spirit will restore passion for prayer, power for witnessing, and purity in our inner being. Don't sit around in mourning and moping; go before the Lord and *ask sincerely for a fresh filling of the Spirit*. Pray just as Jesus instructed: "If you then . . . know how to give good gifts to your children, how much more will your Father in heaven give the Holy Spirit to those who ask him" (Luke 11:13).

A few years ago I received an e-mail from a lady who had been in a revival service where I preached. She wrote, "That revival service surely made a difference in my life! One night you challenged us to come forward and exchange something that was not good—something that was not of God—and trade it for something God wanted to replace it with, something good. Brother, I gave up my sadness, my heaviness, my darkness, and my negative views and fears. And God has given me something I've never known before—joy unspeakable and full of glory!"

Dear Christian reader, do you have the Holy Spirit's fire burning in your heart? Are you abundantly alive with a strong faith in Jesus Christ? Can you freely claim to be walking with God in intimate fellowship? No, I'm not asking you if you are perfect—Jesus is the only perfect human being! But He died that we might have eternal life. And He died for more than that; He suffered for our sins and to purchase abundant life—the *fullness* of the Spirit, the *freedom* of the Spirit, the *fruit* of the Spirit, and the *fire* of the Spirit.

Would you like to trade in a cold heart for a burning heart, a hard heart for a holy heart, a carnal mind for a spiritual mind, a fearful heart for a forceful heart? Then come before the Lord with a humble and honest heart, confessing your needs and pouring out all that has hindered you and held you back from divine fullness and power. God already knows these things, but He wants to hear your honest and humble confession. He wants to hear you *asking Him to impart to you the faith and fire that He promises to help you live a victorious Christian life!*

Please don't be afraid of the Holy Spirit. You can trust Him just as completely as you can trust our Heavenly Father and our Lord Jesus Christ. They are exactly the same in their nature. The fullness of the Holy Spirit will not make you into a fool, a freak, or a fanatic. No, the fullness of the Spirit will take you deeper into Christlikeness, making you more like Jesus. Actually, according to the Scriptures, this was God's purpose in saving you in the first place. The apostle Paul wrote, "And we know that in all things God works for the good of those who love him, who have been called according to his purpose. For those God foreknew he also predestined to be conformed to the likeness of his Son" (Romans 8:28-29). Again, Paul wrote, "Now the Lord is the Spirit, and where the Spirit of the Lord is, there is freedom. And we, who with unveiled faces all reflect the Lord's glory, are being transformed into his likeness with ever-increasing glory, which comes from the Lord, who is the Spirit" (II Corinthians 3:17-18).

Let us ask the Holy Spirit to help us have the hunger, the humility, and the honesty to make a sincere plea for the filling of the Holy Spirit. Remember, we have His promise that if we want the gift of His fullness, we need to ask. So let's ask now!

Prayer: Thank You, Lord, for saving me and giving me Your Holy Spirit. I truly believe Your Spirit lives in me even now. But on the authority of Your Word, I'm coming to You now to confess that I am lacking in faith, in freedom, and in the fullness and fire of the Spirit.

Please, Lord, I don't want to go on living in cold-heartedness, giving in to the weaknesses of carnal desires and bad attitudes. I want the power of love to inspire loving attitudes, holy relationships, and meaningful services toward others. Forgive my critical and judgmental spirit, and replace this with a baptism of divine love.

Oh, God, I want to be Christ-centered, not self-centered! I want to be free in the Spirit, not in bondage to religion! I want to be drawn to Jesus by the Spirit and not swayed by the spirit of the world! Help me get my eyes off others and seek to please You only.

Lord, I'm asking You to fill me with Your Spirit, and I'm believing that You do! Thank You for the fullness of Your presence, the assurance of Your presence, and the joy of Your presence!

And, Lord, if and when I grieve, quench, disobey, ignore, or run past the constraints or restraints of the Holy Spirit, please help me to be immediately sensitive to His convicting presence. Help me to repent immediately and pray for the rekindling and refilling of His presence and power. Amen!

22

The Spirit of Salvation

"I baptize you with water for repentance. But after me will come one who is more powerful than I, whose sandals I am not fit to carry. He will baptize you with the Holy Spirit and with fire. His winnowing fork is in his hand, and he will clear his threshing floor, gathering his wheat into the barn and burning up the chaff with unquenchable fire" (Matthew 3:11-12).

These words from God's anointed forerunner of our Lord Jesus Christ announce a great distinction between the old dispensation of the Law that is closing and the new dispensation of Grace which was about to open. It will be John the Baptist's privilege to introduce "the Lamb of God, who takes away the sin of the world" (John 1:29). John also wanted the people to know that while he had baptized with water Jesus would be the baptizer "with the Holy Spirit and with fire."

    A distinction of the new age of Grace would be the manner and measure in which the Holy Spirit would be poured out on those who believed in the Lord Jesus Christ as the Son of God and who would crown Him as Lord of their lives.

    Of course, the Holy Spirit is the Eternal Spirit just as our Heavenly Father and our Lord Jesus Christ are eternal. And we read of the presence and action of the Holy Spirit on earth even during the creation: "In the beginning God created the heavens and the earth. Now the earth was formless and empty, darkness was over the surface of the deep, and the Spirit of God was hovering over the waters" (Genesis 1:1-2). The Holy Spirit was active in the lives of Old Testament believers, but not to the sanctifying, abiding, and comforting degree we see Him in the Church age.

Just as we see the Holy Spirit active in creation, we also see Him active in the Incarnation: "This is how the birth of Jesus Christ came about: His mother Mary was pledged to be married to Joseph, but before they came together, she was found to be with child through the Holy Spirit" (Matthew 1:18). The angel explained, 'Joseph, son of David, do not be afraid to take Mary home as your wife, because what is conceived in her is from the Holy Spirit. She will give birth to a son, and you are to give him the name Jesus, because he will save his people from their sins'" (Matthew 1:20-21). The Holy Spirit was active in the human life of Jesus. Before Jesus began His public ministry, "the Holy Spirit descended on him" (Luke 3:22). Before preaching, teaching, or working miracles, the Holy Spirit led Jesus into the desert for 40 days of prayer and fasting and to be tempted by the devil (Matthew 4:1-2). Throughout His three years of public ministry, everything Jesus did was done in the power of the Holy Spirit. His final act in which He fulfilled the purpose of His coming was to offer Himself as a sacrifice for our sins. The writer of the book of Hebrews explained the source of His strength for this indescribable act of suffering: "How much more, then, will the blood of Christ, who through the eternal Spirit offered himself unblemished to God, cleanse our consciences from acts that lead to death, so that we may serve the living God" (Hebrews 9:14).

Even before His crucifixion, Jesus spent time promising the coming of the Holy Spirit upon His believers and explaining the Spirit's role in their lives (John, chapters 14-16). As He departed to be with the Father in Heaven, Jesus' final words to His apostles were to go back into the city of Jerusalem and tarry for the Spirit's coming. The present age since the Pentecostal outpouring of the Holy Spirit (Acts 2:1-4) has been referred to as "The Age of the Holy Spirit."

But the Spirit Himself inspired the apostle Paul to call attention to the supremacy of Jesus Christ: "He is the image of the invisible God, the firstborn over all creation. For by him all things were created: things in heaven and on earth, visible and invisible, whether thrones or powers or rulers or authorities; all things were created by him and for him. He is before all things, and in him all things hold together. And he is the head of the body, the church; he is the beginning and the firstborn from among the dead, so that in everything he might have the supremacy. For God was pleased to have all his fullness dwell in him, and through him to reconcile to himself all things, whether things on earth or things in heaven, by making peace through his blood, shed on the cross" (Colossians 1:15-20).

In preparing His disciples for the coming of the Holy Spirit, Jesus made it clear that there could be no salvation apart from the work of the Holy Spirit. Jesus Himself purchased our salvation with His blood, but it would require the convicting work of the Holy Spirit to bring each penitent believer into spiritual regeneration—the new birth. The Spirit actually comes to abide in the born-again believer. Learning to relate to the Holy Spirit is the secret of the Christian's victorious life of faith.

The Holy Spirit is not only the Spirit of regeneration; He is also the Spirit of sanctification. The apostle Paul was concerned that the Gospel would be appropriately proclaimed "so that the Gentiles might become an offering acceptable to God, sanctified by the Holy Spirit" (Romans 15:16). The same apostle reminded the Thessalonians that "from the beginning God chose you to be saved through the sanctifying work of the Spirit and through belief in the truth" (II Thessalonians 2:13).

To the same believers he wrote, "May God himself, the God of peace, sanctify you through and through. May your whole spirit, soul and body be kept blameless at the coming of our Lord Jesus Christ. The one who calls you is faithful and he will do it" (I Thessalonians 5:23-24).

I've noticed a dullness in the thinking of too many believers regarding the need of going beyond the experience of the new birth and moving on to "grow in the grace and knowledge of our Lord and Savior Jesus Christ" (II Peter 3:18). The Holy Spirit indwelling the new believer will always inspire the hunger for cleansing, growth, maturity, and perseverance. But we believers have an enemy who seeks to distract, discourage, and defeat us in our walk with God. Satan hates the work of salvation; even after we have believed, he seeks to rob us of our passion for righteousness and holiness. For this reason, God's Word calls us to become sensitive to the Spirit's call: "Today, if you hear his voice, do not harden your hearts" (Hebrews 4:7).

Sanctification is the divine act of cleansing from sin in the heart of the believer, and this begins in the new birth experience. But, at some point during the early life of our Christian experience we'll feel the Spirit's call to the total surrender of our lives to Jesus, in which we make Him *Lord* of our lives. This experience comes subsequent to the regeneration experience, and heart purity is the essence of the occasion—a uniting of the inner man's being in a total consecration to Christ. This results in the removal of the double-mindedness, and the believer is enabled by life in the Spirit to hold to a daily single-heartedness in devotion to Jesus Christ.

But while we are to rejoice in the crisis experience of sanctification, let us remember that we are called to a progressive sanctification by the apostle Paul who wrote, "And all of us, with unveiled faces, seeing the glory of the Lord as though reflected in a mirror, are being transformed into the same image from one degree of glory to another; for this comes from the Lord, the Spirit" (II Corinthians 3:18, NRSV). There is a sense in which an obedient believer may say, "I *have been* sanctified." And there is also a sense in which an obedient believer may say, "I am *being sanctified*." We may be sure that God has predestined us "to be conformed to the likeness of his Son" (Romans 8:29). Living the sanctified life is nothing less and nothing more than continually growing more and more like Jesus Christ.

Prayer: Lord, thank You for dying to save me and to make me holy. Also, thank You for sending Your Holy Spirit to mold me continually into Your likeness. I confess that I sometimes fall short of being like Jesus. But when I do and the Spirit convicts me, I confess my sin. I have Your promise that "If we confess our sins, he is faithful and just and will forgive us our sins and purify us from all unrighteousness" (I John 1:9).

Lord, enable me to think, pray, and live in the power of the Spirit, because Your Word declares that "through Christ Jesus the law of the Spirit of life sets me free from the law of sin and death" (Romans 8:2). I thank You that I'm not living under the Law but under grace by fellowship with You through the indwelling presence of the Holy Spirit.

Thank You, Lord, for the Spirit of salvation who saves, sanctifies, and abides faithfully within me. Amen!

23

The Holy Spirit and the Second Coming of Christ

"But about that day and hour no one knows, neither the angels of heaven, nor the Son, but only the Father. For as the days of Noah were, so will be the coming of the Son of Man. For as in those days before the flood they were eating and drinking, marrying and giving in marriage, until the day Noah entered the ark, and they knew nothing until the flood came and swept them all away, so too will be the coming of the Son of Man. Then two will be in the field; one will be taken and one will be left. Two women will be grinding meal together; one will be taken and one will be left. Keep awake therefore, for you do not know on what day your Lord is coming. But understand this: if the owner of the house had known in what part of the night the thief was coming, he would have stayed awake and would not have let his house be broken into. Therefore you also must be ready, for the Son of Man is coming at an unexpected hour" (Matthew 24:36-44, NRSV).

"He who has an ear, let him hear what the Spirit says to the churches" (Revelation 2:29).

From the very hour in which our Lord Jesus Christ was caught up in His ascension to the Father, Christian believers everywhere have rejoiced in their hope of His promised Second Coming. The apostles watched Jesus ascend, and then He was out of sight. ". . . suddenly, two men in white robes stood by them. They said, 'Men of Galilee, why do you stand looking up toward heaven? This Jesus, who has been taken up from you into heaven, will come in the same way as you saw him go into heaven'" (Acts 1:10-11, NRSV).

Surely, Christ's Second Coming is of the utmost importance to all believers. But we must give attention to all that Jesus and His apostles said about our preparation for His Coming. In order to be ready, every one of us must have the help of the Holy Spirit, who dwells within us.

We learn from Jesus and His apostles that the Second Coming will have two phases. In the first phase, He will come to rapture ("catch away") His Bride. The world and those unready for His appearance will not see Him. "For the Lord Himself will descend from heaven with a shout, with the voice of an archangel, and with the trumpet of God. And the dead in Christ will rise first. Then we who are alive *and* remain shall be caught up together with them in the clouds to meet the Lord in the air. And thus we shall always be with the Lord" (I Thessalonians 4:16-17, NKJV).

The second phase of the Second Coming will be a Revelation: "Behold, He is coming with clouds, and every eye will see Him, even they who pierced Him. And all the tribes of the earth will mourn because of Him" (Revelation 1:7, NKJV). Jesus will return from the very place from which He ascended—to the Mount of Olives in a great earthquake. "On that day his feet will stand on the Mount of Olives, east of Jerusalem, and the Mount of Olives will be split in two from east to west, forming a great valley, with half of the mountain moving north and half moving south" (Zechariah 14:4). Jesus Himself confirmed Zechariah's prophecy by saying, "For as the lightning comes from the east and flashes to the west, so also will the coming of the Son of Man be. . . . Then the sign of the Son of Man will appear in heaven, and then all the tribes of the earth will mourn, and they will see the Son of Man coming on the clouds of heaven with power and great glory" (Matthew 24:27,30, NKJV).

The earth to which Jesus returns in the second phase of His Coming will be to one filled with tragedy and sorrow because of divine wrath on the multitudes who have rejected His Son and believed the lies of the Antichrist. The apostle Paul predicted that believers living on earth just before Christ's return would be affected by bold incursions of evil spirits commissioned by the Antichrist. "The coming of the lawless one will be in accordance with the work of Satan displayed in all kinds of counterfeit miracles, signs and wonders, and in every sort of evil that deceives those who are perishing. They perish because they refused to love the truth and so be saved. For this reason God sends them a powerful delusion so that they will believe the lie and so that all will be condemned who have not believed the truth but have delighted in wickedness" (II Thessalonians 2:9-12).

With all the love of His great heart Jesus passionately warns us to be prepared for His Coming. He warns us that there will be no bulletins announcing the time of His Coming, no calls from Heaven making appointments. *We must be ready!*

Now I cannot believe that Jesus wants all of His born-again followers to walk around in paralyzed fear that we will miss the Rapture. But He and His apostles made it clear that in order to be ready for His Coming we must be walking in fellowship with an ungrieved, unquenched Holy Spirit. We do this by walking in the Spirit, praying in the Spirit, loving one another, encouraging one another to live in holiness and power, and allowing the Spirit to search our hearts, convict us of sin and selfishness, and bring us to repentance, cleansing, and spiritual renewal.

Our Savior knew exactly what the times would be like before He returned. So He said: "The sky and the earth (that is, the universe, the world) will pass away; but My words will not pass away. But take heed to yourselves *and* be on your guard lest your hearts be overburdened and depressed (weighed down) with the giddiness *and* headache *and* nausea of self-indulgence, drunkenness, and worldly worries *and* cares pertaining to [the business of] this life, and that day come upon you suddenly like a trap *or* a noose; For it will come upon all who live upon the face of the entire earth. Keep awake then *and* watch at all times [that is, be discreet, attentive and ready]; praying that you may have the full strength *and* ability *and* be accounted worthy to escape all these things [taken together] that will take place, and to stand in the presence of the Son of man" (Luke 21:33-36, AMP).

Consider the conditions that Jesus condemned in five of the seven churches in Revelation 2:1—3:22. Ephesus, Pergamum, Thyatira,

Sardis, and Laodicea were called upon to *repent*. But the believers in all seven churches, including Smyrna and Philadelphia, were warned. "He who has an ear, let him hear what the Spirit says to the churches" (Revelation 2:7).

- Ephesus received the shocking news that it had left its first love (Revelation 2:4).

- Pergamum was charged with embracing the doctrine of Balaam (Revelation 2:14).

- Thyatira tolerated the spirit of Jezebel in sexually defiling the members of the church (Revelation 2:20).

- Sardis was filled with nominal Christians and had a reputation of being alive, but was dead (Revelation 3:1).

- Laodicea was neither cold nor hot, and its indifference made the Lord sick (Revelation 3:15-16).

Our Lord's message to these five churches made it clear that they were not ready for His Coming unless they *repented*. They could not stand before Him in their present state. But He was ready to forgive, cleanse, renew, and restore them to the joy and hope of their salvation if they had an ear to hear what the Spirit was revealing.

My Christian friends, we must allow the Holy Spirit to lead us to pray, "Have mercy upon me, O God, according to Your loving-kindness; according to the multitude of Your tender mercies, blot out my transgressions. Wash me thoroughly from my iniquity, and cleanse me from my sin" (Psalm 51:1-2, NKJV). "Create in me a clean heart, O God, and renew a steadfast spirit within me. Do not cast me away from Your presence, and do not take Your Holy Spirit from me. Restore to me the joy of Your salvation, and uphold me *by Your generous Spirit*" (Psalm 51:10-12, NKJV).

Our Lord and Savior wants us to walk in the assurance of His indwelling Holy Spirit so that we shall be caught up with Him at His Coming. So let each of us pray with the apostle Paul: "May God himself, the God who makes everything holy and whole, make (me) holy and whole, put (me) together—spirit, soul, and body—and keep (me) fit for the coming of our Master, Jesus Christ. The One who called (me) is completely dependable. If he said it, he will do it" (I Thessalonians 5:23-24, The Message).

Prayer: Heavenly Father, thank You for sending Your one and only Son Jesus to die an atoning death for all our sins. And thank You, Lord Jesus, for promising to send the Holy Spirit to convict us of sin, to comfort us in our times of sorrow and stress, and to counsel us in our weaknesses and ignorance.

O Lord, thank You for the faithfulness of the Holy Spirit to prompt us when we fall short of Your will and Your way. We must not give in to the evil one's subtle attempts to distract us from walking in the Spirit and being ready for the return of our Lord. We cannot stay alert without the help of Your Spirit.

Help us to walk in the daily assurance of the sanctifying presence of the Holy Spirit. Help us walk in the fellowship of an ungrieved, unquenched Holy Spirit and be ready for the Coming of the Lord whether He comes for us in death or in the rapture. Amen!

24

The Seal of the Spirit

"In Him you also trusted, after you heard the word of truth, the gospel of your salvation; in whom also, having believed, you were sealed with the Holy Spirit of promise, who is the guarantee of our inheritance until the redemption of the purchased possession, to the praise of His glory" (Ephesians 1:13-14, NKJV).

The first three chapters of the apostle Paul's epistle to the Ephesians is one continuous doxology in prayer. He is inspired by the Holy Spirit to reveal the grace and glory of our Creator-Redeemer in His plan of salvation for the fallen human race. In order to give some structure to what the apostle referred to as our inheritance, let us consider: *the power of the Gospel, God's purpose in redemption,* and *the promise of the Spirit's seal.*

The Power of the Gospel

The apostle Paul testified, "I am not ashamed of the gospel, because it is the power of God for the salvation of everyone who believes" (Romans 1:16). In the gospel we see the power of the Holy Trinity—God the Father planned our salvation, God the Son purchased our salvation, and God the Holy Spirit administers our salvation.

The power of divine *love* is the primary factor in the gospel of our salvation. Jesus told Nicodemus that "God so loved the world that he gave his one and only Son, that whoever believes in him shall not perish but have eternal life. For God did not send his Son into the world to condemn the world, but to save the world through him. Whoever believes in him is not condemned, but whoever does not believe stands condemned already because he has not believed in the name of God's one and only Son" (John 3:16-18).

The apostle John declared that "God is love" (I John 4:16). Our Heavenly Father is the source of love, and it was this very power that He so extravagantly demonstrated when He sent His Son, Jesus Christ, into the world to suffer and die for our salvation. The apostle explained it this way: "This is how God showed his love among us: He sent his one and only Son into the world that we might live through him" and sent his Son as an atoning sacrifice for our sins (I John 4:9-10).

But if divine love is the primary factor in the good news of our salvation, there must also be the human response of *faith*. Jesus said, "whoever believes in him shall not perish but have eternal life." Believing is trusting, relying upon, and counting completely on. The apostle Paul wrote, "For it is by grace you have been saved, through faith—and this not from yourselves, it is the gift of God—not by works, so that no one can boast" (Ephesians 2:8-9). We cannot save ourselves. Doing good works is not the *cause* of our salvation; it is the *effect* of our salvation.

If we respond to God's love in Christ by faith, we are then "born of the Spirit" (John 3:8). The Spirit breathes into the believing heart the spiritual life that Jesus promised when He declared, "I am the way and the truth and the life. No one comes to the Father except through me" (John 14:6).

God's Purpose in Redemption

Our Heavenly Father knew that Adam and Eve would fail their moral test in the Garden of Eden. But the apostle Paul declared that God's plan from the beginning was to redeem and reshape believers into the likeness of His Son, Jesus Christ: "For he chose us in him before the creation of the world to be holy and blameless in his sight. In love he predestined us to be adopted as his sons through Jesus Christ, in accordance with his pleasure and will" (Ephesians 1:4-5).

It is clear in both the teachings of Jesus and in the writings of His apostles that the Father's redeemed family was to become like their Savior, the Son of God, Jesus Christ. We were to become His disciples—followers, learners, ambassadors. His Spirit within us would shape us into His likeness. "And we, who with unveiled faces all reflect the Lord's glory, are being transformed into his likeness with ever-increasing glory, which comes from the Lord, who is the Spirit" (II Corinthians 3:18). Again, we were predestined by our Eternal Father "to be conformed to the likeness of his Son" (Romans 8:29).

In order for us to be made into the likeness of Jesus, we are given the Holy Spirit in our new birth experience. As we walk in fellowship with an ungrieved Holy Spirit, He becomes our Convictor of sin, our Sanctifier from sin, our Counselor in truth, and our Comforter throughout life.

The born-again believer is commanded to live "not by the sinful nature but by the Spirit. . . . And if the Spirit of him who raised Jesus from the dead is living in you, he who raised Christ from the dead will also give life to your mortal bodies through His Spirit, who lives in you" (Romans 8:9,11).

Christian believers are called to fulfill the will of God by living their daily lives in the fullness of power through the Holy Spirit—to pray in the Spirit, think in the Spirit, and make decisions in light of the Spirit's approval and disapproval. They are to relate intimately with the Holy Spirit, even as the disciples related to Jesus during their three years with Him—learning, worshiping, praying, and obeying.

The Promise of the Spirit's Seal

The apostle Paul reviews the history of the Ephesian believers by acknowledging their hearing of the gospel and their receiving of the gospel by believing. Now he is ready to remind them of a glorious inheritance that came with their new birth in Christ: "Having believed, you were marked in him [Christ] with a seal, the promised Holy Spirit, who is a deposit guaranteeing our inheritance until the redemption of those who are God's possession—to the praise of his glory" (Ephesians 1:13-14).

In Paul's time, letters, contracts, and other important documents were stamped by the owners or signers by pressing their seal into warm wax, thereby revealing their identification and ownership. One who has been born of the Spirit is stamped by the Holy Spirit as adopted into the family of God. Our Heavenly Father has bought us. "Do you not know that your body is a temple of the Holy Spirit, who is in you, whom you have received from God? You are not your own; you were bought at a price" (I Corinthians 6:19-20). "For you know that it was not with perishable things such as silver or gold that you were redeemed from the empty way of life handed down to you from your forefathers, but with the precious blood of Christ, a lamb without blemish or defect. He was chosen before the creation of the world, but was revealed in these last times for your sake. Through him you believe in God, who raised him from the dead and glorified him, and so your faith and hope are in God" (I Peter 1:18-21).

We need to see at least two things in the *sealing of the Spirit:* divine ownership and divine assurance. As born-again children of God we have been adopted into the family of God. The very quality of our inheritance is stamped on our human spirit. Consequently, we relate to Him in fellowship—prayer, praise, worship, obedience, and in glorious anticipation of our Savior's return for us in either death or the rapture.

But the Holy Spirit within us is also "the guarantee of our inheritance" (Ephesians 1:14, NKJV)—a down payment on what is to come in the end—glorification and an eternal abode with our Heavenly Father and our Lord Jesus Christ.

Three times we have an expression in divine worship in the terms *"Abba, Father!"* The first is when our Lord agonized in worshipful surrender to the Father's will in Gethsemane. He willed the Father's will—He would die on the cross (Mark 14:36); the second is when the apostle Paul is explaining the manner in which Christian believers pour out their praise and affection for the Heavenly Father, realizing their family membership (Romans 8:15); and the third is the same apostle's similar description to the Roman believers in their worship as they realize that the Father has "sent the Spirit of his Son into (their) hearts" (Galatians 4:6). It is the Spirit who inspires this depth of worship.

Prayer: Oh, Glorious Father, thank You that "while we were still sinners, Christ died for us." How gracious and merciful You have been to choose us for salvation long before we chose to confess Your Son as our Savior. Heavenly Father and Lord Jesus, You have been so gracious in giving us Your very Spirit to convict, comfort, and counsel us and to help us understand Your Word, know Your will, and grow in your love and grace!

Please help us understand what awaits us as we continue to walk with the Spirit in holiness, power, worship, and witness. We are anticipating our eternal future—being caught up with Christ in a resurrected, glorified body; reuniting with loved ones gone on before; the Marriage Supper of the Lamb; and a new heaven and a new earth and our place in it!

How we praise You for the seal of the Spirit! Amen! And Amen!

25

The Holy Spirit as "The Finger of God"

"Then they brought him a demon-possessed man who was blind and mute, and Jesus healed him, so that he could both talk and see. All the people were astonished and said, 'Could this be the Son of David?'

"But when the Pharisees heard this, they said, 'It is by Beelzebub, the prince of demons, that this fellow drives out demons.'

"Jesus knew their thoughts and said to them, 'Every kingdom divided against itself will be ruined, and every city or household divided against itself will not stand. If Satan drives out Satan, he is divided against himself. How then can his kingdom stand? And if I drive out demons by Beelzebub, by whom do your people drive them out? So then, they will be your judges. But if I drive out demons by the Spirit of God, then the kingdom of God has come upon you'" (Matthew 12:22-28).

The rejection and anger of the Pharisees against Jesus was so atrocious that they accused him of being possessed by Satanic powers. They could not deny his miraculous works—the blind saw, the mute spoke, and the lame walked. So the enemies of Jesus decided to attribute his source of power to Beelzebub, the prince of demons.

Before pronouncing judgment on their blasphemy, Jesus exposed their illogical arguments—not even the agents of an evil kingdom operate against their own purposes. Then He went on to identify His source of power as the "Spirit of God" (v. 28). In the synagogue where he had been raised Jesus identified the source of his authority: "The Spirit of the Lord is on me, because he has anointed me to preach good news to the poor. He has sent me to proclaim freedom for the prisoners and recovery of sight for the blind, to release the oppressed, to proclaim the year of the Lord's favor" (Luke 4:18-19).

The phrase "the finger of God" appears for the first time in Exodus 8:19. God told Moses and Aaron that when Pharaoh tells you to perform a miracle you (Moses) tell Aaron to throw down his staff before Pharaoh. When Aaron did this, his staff became a serpent. Astonished, Pharaoh brought out his magicians to do the same thing. To the amazement of Moses and Aaron, the magicians' staffs also became serpents. But there was a glorious difference: Aaron's staff swallowed up the magicians' staffs.

But there is more to the story. In chapter 8 of Exodus, Aaron called forth the plague of gnats by striking the dust of the ground; the dust became gnats. When the Egyptian wizards could not imitate the miracles of Moses and Aaron, they went to Pharaoh and said of the power of God's men, "This is the finger of God" (Exodus 8:19).

The phrase appears dramatically again in Exodus 31:18: "When the Lord finished speaking to Moses on Mount Sinai, he gave him the two tablets of the Testimony, the tablets of stone inscribed by the finger of God." By this we know that the Holy Spirit inspired the Old Testament. And we are assured the same is true of the New covenant: "All scripture is inspired by God and is useful for teaching, for reproof, for correction, and for training in righteousness, so that everyone who belongs to God may be proficient, equipped for every good work" (II Timothy 3:16-17, NRSV).

Jesus spent more time with His disciples on the subject of the Holy Spirit than He did on any other subject. He knew they could never make true and successful followers of His if they did not know the power of the Holy Spirit. On His departure, their first order of business was to go back into the city and "stay . . . until you have been clothed with power from on high" (Luke 24:49). "John baptized with water, but in a few days you will be baptized with the Holy Spirit" (Acts 1:5). "But you will receive power when the Holy Spirit comes on you; and you will be my witnesses in Jerusalem, and in all Judea and Samaria, and to the ends of the earth" (Acts 1:8).

The disciples obeyed the command immediately on their Master's ascension to Heaven. "They returned to Jerusalem from the hill called the Mount of Olives, a Sabbath day's walk from the city. When they arrived, they went upstairs to the room where they were staying. . . . They all joined together constantly in prayer, along with the women and Mary the mother of Jesus, and with his brothers" (Acts 1:12-14).

After about ten days of praying, Luke tells us what happened: "When the day of Pentecost came, they were all together in one place. Suddenly a sound like the blowing of a violent wind came from heaven and filled the whole house where they were sitting. They saw what seemed to be tongues of fire that separated and came to rest on each of them. All of them were filled with the Holy Spirit and began to speak in other tongues as the Spirit enabled them" (Acts 2:1-4).

Filled with the Holy Spirit, the 120 believers filed out of the Upper Room and went down to street level where thousands of pilgrims mingled with dwellers in Jerusalem preparing to celebrate the Feast of Pentecost. When the crowd heard the Spirit-filled believers "declaring the wonders of God" in all the languages represented, they were "amazed and perplexed" and "asked one another, 'What does this mean?'" (Acts 2:5-12).

"Then Peter stood up with the Eleven" and explained what had happened to them as prophesied by the prophet Joel. He declared that God had sent Jesus to save mankind, but then he accused them, saying, ". . . you, with the help of wicked men, put him to death by nailing him to the cross. But God raised him from the dead" (Acts 2:14-24).

The "Finger of God" was not only upon the anointed apostle to proclaim Christ's atoning death for our sins, but this same Holy Spirit was on the crowd of thousands in conviction of sin: "When the people heard this, they were cut to the heart and said to Peter and the other apostles, 'Brothers, what shall we do?' (Acts 2:37).

"Peter replied, 'Repent and be baptized, every one of you, in the name of Jesus Christ for the forgiveness of your sins. And you will receive the gift of the Holy Spirit. The promise is for you and your children and for all who are far off—for all whom our God will call.'

With many other words he warned them; and he pleaded with them, 'Save yourselves from this corrupt generation'" (Acts 2:38-40).

"The finger of God" was upon Peter and also upon the crowd, for the historian Luke reports that "those who accepted his message were baptized, and about three thousand were added to their number that day" (Acts 2:41).

The remaining verses of chapter 2 of Luke assure that "the finger of God" became the secret of the growth and power of the early church: "They devoted themselves to the apostles' teaching and to the fellowship, to the breaking of bread and to prayer. Everyone was filled with awe, and many wonders and miraculous signs were done by the apostles. All the believers were together and had everything in common. Selling their possessions and goods, they gave to anyone as he had need. Every day they continued to meet together in the temple courts. They broke bread in their homes and ate together with glad and sincere hearts, praising God and enjoying the favor of all the people. And the Lord added to their number daily those who were being saved" (Acts 2:42-47).

Neither the Christian believers nor the unbelievers noticing the marvelous happenings among the new members of the body of Christ in Jerusalem could deny that "the finger of God" was upon them. They were filled with love for one another, which Jesus had said that love would be the true badge of Christian discipleship: "A new command I give you: Love one another. As I have loved you, so you must love one another. By this all men will know that you are my disciples, if you love one another" (John 13:34-35). This meant that they cared, respected, valued, and supported one another and refrained from judgmentalism and criticism. When the unsaved came among them, they left with their hearts desiring such inner peace and joy.

The early Christians made certain that their unsaved guests knew the source of their transformed lives—"the finger of God." It is not surprising that "the Lord added to their number daily those who were being saved."

The same is true today where born-again, Spirit-filled believers worship and fellowship. Their love for their Savior and each other is attractive, appealing, and infectious.

Among genuine believers there is no need or excuse for proselytizing. The Gospel of Jesus Christ is good news to saint and sinner, old and young, rich and poor, black and white, and learned and unlearned. This is true, especially when unbelievers see the love, joy, and peace in the lives of those who know Jesus Christ.

Prayer: Father, thank You for the promise of the Holy Spirit. We are learning that there is power in thinking, praying, and living under the influence of this special Guest You have sent to live within us—Your very Spirit and Your Son's very Spirit. We thank You for this inner power, peace, and presence that makes a difference in our daily lives.

Help me, Lord, to be sensitive to the people around me and those You bring into my influence. Help me respond to them with the radiance of Your love and testify to them lovingly about Your mercy and grace in saving me. May I be free to appeal to them to turn in faith to such a wonderful Savior and enjoy "the finger of God" in their own lives. Please give me a greater love for the lost. Amen!

26

The Spirit of Life

"I tell you the truth, no one can enter the kingdom of God unless he is born of water and the Spirit. Flesh gives birth to flesh, but the Spirit gives birth to spirit" (John 3:5-6).

"Therefore, there is now no condemnation for those who are in Christ Jesus, because through Christ Jesus the law of the Spirit of life set me free from the law of sin and death" (Romans 8:1-2).

"The Spirit gives life; the flesh counts for nothing. The words I have spoken to you are spirit and they are life" (John 6:63).

"He has made us competent as ministers of a new covenant—not of the letter but of the Spirit; for the letter kills, but the Spirit gives life" (II Corinthians 3:6).

Jesus Christ declared Himself to be "the way and the truth and the life" (John 14:6). After dying for our sins, He ascended to the Father and His promise to send the Holy Spirit, the very Spirit of the Father and the Son, was fulfilled on the Day of Pentecost (Acts 2:1-4). Jesus told Nicodemus that "no one can enter the kingdom of God unless he is born of water and the Spirit. Flesh gives birth to flesh, but the Spirit gives birth to spirit" (John 3:5-6). In our natural birth we inherit the sin of Adam, and no amount of good works will qualify us for an entrance into the kingdom of God. Jesus made it clear to Nicodemus that only a new birth of and by the Holy Spirit will allow us to enter the Kingdom of God. Paul the apostle reminded the Ephesian believers: "As for you, you were dead in your transgressions and sins, in which you used to live when you followed the ways of this world and of the ruler of the kingdom of the air, the spirit who is now at work in those who are disobedient. All of us also lived among them at one time, gratifying the cravings of our sinful nature and following its desires and thoughts. Like the rest, we were by nature objects of wrath. But because of his great love for us, God, who is rich in mercy, made us alive with Christ even when we were dead in transgressions—it is by grace you have been saved" (Ephesians 2:1-5).

We born-again believers have had a spiritual resurrection by the power of the Holy Spirit, who is the Spirit of life. We were generated in the flesh by our parents; we are regenerated by the Holy Spirit. The same apostle explained this again by noting the amazing spiritual transformation of regeneration: "At one time we too were foolish, disobedient, deceived and enslaved by all kinds of passions and pleasures. We lived in malice and envy, being hated and hating one another. But when the kindness and love of God our Savior appeared, he saved us, not because of righteous things we had done, but because of his mercy. He saved us through the washing of rebirth and renewal by the Holy Spirit, whom he poured out on us generously through Jesus Christ our Savior, so that, having been justified by his grace, we might become heirs having the hope of eternal life" (Titus 3:3-7).

Regeneration is a spiritual miracle wrought in the heart of the penitent sinner who has come under the convicting power of the Holy Spirit. In promising the Spirit, Jesus said, "When he comes, he will convict the world of guilt in regard to sin and righteousness and judgment; in regard to sin, because men do not believe in me" (John 16:8-9). Actually, we are told by the apostle Paul that "no one can say, 'Jesus is Lord,' except by the Holy Spirit" (I Corinthians 12:3). The apostle is referring here to the sinner's saving confession of Christ as Savior and Lord. Under the influence of the Spirit's conviction of sin— the sin of not believing in Jesus—the Spirit will lead the penitent sinner to believe the gospel of salvation and receive eternal life.

Through our earthly parents we inherit biological life, which is but a comparatively short span in time on earth. Because of Jesus Christ's atoning death on the cross, the Holy Spirit comes to us and conditions our heart for repentance of sin and faith in Christ for our salvation. The amazing truth is that we are given eternal life.

In our natural state of the flesh, we all know that death will come. But those who have responded to the Holy Spirit's conviction of sin by repenting and confessing Christ as Savior and Lord will live forever. The born-again, believing follower of Jesus Christ survives death. Hear the apostle's hope expressed for all of us to read: "Now we know that if the earthly tent we live in is destroyed, we have a building from God, an eternal house in heaven, not built by human hands" (II Corinthians 5:1). All believers should hold the hopeful perspective of the apostle Paul who wrote, "But we have this treasure in jars of clay to show that this all-surpassing power is from God and not from us. We are hard-pressed on every side, but not crushed; perplexed, but not in despair; persecuted, but not abandoned; struck down, but not destroyed. We always carry around in our body the death of Jesus, so that the life of Jesus may also be revealed in our body" (II Corinthians 4:7-10). "Therefore we do not lose heart. Though outwardly we are wasting away, yet inwardly we are being renewed day by day. For our light and momentary troubles are achieving for us an eternal glory that far outweighs them all. So we fix our eyes not on what is seen, but on what is unseen. For what is seen is temporary, but what is unseen is eternal" (II Corinthians 4:16-18).

While we are called to rejoice in our hope of what is eternal, or that which is to come, let us not ignore the power and glory of the abundant life that God has promised believers during this our journey toward the eternal. Not only do we have eternal life the moment we are born again, but the born-again believer is called to *abundant life*. Jesus promised, "I have come that they may have life, and have it to the full" (John 10:10).

Abundant life in Christ includes being *filled with the Spirit*. Of course, believers receive the Holy Spirit in the experience of the new birth. But it is clear in the teachings of Jesus and His New Testament writers that we are not to remain newly-born babes in Christ. When visiting the Corinthians, the apostle Paul was disappointed to find the lack of growth. In I Corinthians 3:1-3 he says, "Brothers, I could not address you as spiritual but as worldly—mere infants in Christ. I gave you milk, not solid food, for you were not yet ready for it. Indeed, you are still not ready. You are still worldly. For since there is jealousy and quarreling among you, are you not worldly? Are you not acting like mere men?" Paul continued to point out their carnality—their division, immaturity, and immorality. They may have begun in Christ, but they certainly were not continuing in Him. They were not even fellowshipping with and blessing one another; they had nothing attractive within their church body that would appeal to the world.

The new birth means that those young in the faith hunger for the milk of the Word. They learn from the Scriptures the truths of true discipleship and about growing in the grace and in the knowledge of our Lord and Savior Jesus Christ. Sooner or later, the faithful new convert will hear and feel the call to the Spirit-filled life. Receiving the Spirit as an unsought gift in the new birth does not mean that we are automatically filled with the Spirit. "Be filled with the Spirit" (Ephesians 5:18) was the apostle Paul's imperative command to the Philippian believers. We move into the abundant life in the power of the Spirit. Jesus said, "But you will receive power when the Holy Spirit comes on you" (Acts 1:8). The Holy Spirit was a given in the new birth, but early in practicing the Christian life there comes the sense of need for *more* of the Spirit, *the fullness of the Spirit*. And Jesus has a promise for those who reach this point: "If you then, though you are evil, know how to give good gifts to your children, how much more will your Father in heaven give the Holy Spirit to those who ask him" (Luke 11:13). The emphasis here is on *asking*.

In praying for the fullness of the Holy Spirit, we must remember another condition we must meet for the filling of the Spirit—*obeying*. Peter and the apostles told their persecutors in Jerusalem, "We are witnesses of these things, and so is the Holy Spirit, whom God has given to those who obey him" (Acts 5:32). The obedient, believing, hungry, surrendered, asking believer receives the fullness of the Holy Spirit.

The evidence of the fullness of the Spirit is *power*—*power* to bear the fruit of the Spirit, *power* to pray, *power* to live a holy life, *power* to witness, and *power* to worship:

- *Power to bear the fruit of the Spirit*: "love, joy, peace, patience, kindness, goodness, faithfulness, gentleness and self-control" (Galatians 5:22-23).

- *Power to pray.* "In the same way, the Spirit helps us in our weakness. We do not know what we ought to pray for, but the Spirit himself intercedes for us with groans that words cannot express. And he who searches our hearts knows the mind of the Spirit, because the Spirit intercedes for the saints in accordance with God's will" (Romans 8:26-27).

- *Power to live a holy life.* "It is God's will that you should be sanctified: that you should avoid sexual immorality; that each of you should learn to control his own body in a way that is holy and honorable, not in passionate lust like the heathen, who do not know God; and that in this matter no one should wrong his brother or take advantage of him. The Lord will punish men for all such sins, as we have already told you and warned you. For God did not call us to be impure, but to live a holy life. Therefore, he who rejects this instruction does not reject man but God, who gives you his Holy Spirit" (I Thessalonians 4:3-8).

- *Power to witness.* "But you will receive power when the Holy Spirit comes on you; and you will be my witnesses in Jerusalem, and in all Judea and Samaria, and to the ends of the earth" (Acts 1:8).

- *Power to worship.* "God *is* Spirit, and those who worship Him must worship in spirit and truth" (John 4:24, NKJV). Jesus worshiped His Heavenly Father with the inspiration of the Holy Spirit. Luke reports, "At that time Jesus, full of joy through the Holy Spirit, said, 'I praise you, Father, Lord of heaven and earth' . . ." (Luke 10:21). Our Lord is the perfect example for all His followers to come alive in the Spirit for divine worship. The Spirit within us longs to bring each of us to the fullness of His power for loving and worshiping our Lord Jesus Christ as "the head of the body, the church; he is the beginning and the firstborn from among the dead, so that in everything he might have the supremacy. For God was pleased to have all his fullness dwell in him, and through him to reconcile to himself all things, whether things on earth or things in heaven, by making peace through his blood, shed on the cross" (Colossians 1:18-20).

<u>Prayer</u>: Our God and Father, thank You for sending Your one and only Son Jesus to atone for our sins and raise us from our spiritual graves. Our hearts that were once dead in trespasses and sin have been resurrected and illuminated by the light and life of the same Spirit Who raised Jesus from the tomb. And now we pray for the power to radiate that glorious light and life to a lost world. Just as Jesus was the light of the world, so He has charged us to shine in this present darkness. Convict us with Your Word that reminds us, "For you were once darkness, but now you are light in the Lord. Live as children of light (for the fruit of the light consists in all goodness, righteousness and truth) and find out what pleases the Lord. Have nothing to do with the fruitless deeds of darkness, but rather expose them. For it is shameful even to mention what the disobedient do in secret. But everything exposed by the light becomes visible, for it is light that makes everything visible. This is why it is said: 'Wake up, O sleeper, rise from the dead, and Christ will shine on you'" (Ephesians 5:8-14).

Lord Jesus, thank You for sharing Your love, Your life, and Your light with me. Please, Lord, rekindle the fire of the Holy Spirit within me, and refine my inner being in order that I might worship You with all my heart and guard against the coldness, blindness, and hardness with which the world, the flesh, and the devil would seek to ensnare me.

Holy Spirit, shine the love of Christ through me when I'm among my brothers and sisters in Christ, and help me radiate Your love and life to a lost world. Amen!

27

The Spirit of Jesus

"Now the Lord is the Spirit, and where the Spirit of the Lord is, there is freedom. And we, who with unveiled faces all reflect the Lord's glory, are being transformed into his likeness with ever-increasing glory, which comes from the Lord, who is the Spirit" (II Corinthians 3:17-18).

When the Son of God became man, He gave up all the prerogatives and privileges of deity. Even though He emptied Himself of His former exalted state, He became the God-man. In His self-emptying, He trusted the Father's plan for perfect success in His redemptive mission. As John testified, "the one whom God has sent speaks the words of God, for God gives the Spirit without limit" (John 3:34). Since the Father could trust Jesus in His human perfection, He gave Him an unlimited measure of the Holy Spirit. And just like all human beings, He was fully dependent on the Spirit for all His works—miracles, teachings, and sufferings. The writer of the Hebrew epistle tells us that it was by the power of the Holy Spirit that Jesus endured the traumatic suffering of Calvary's cross: "How much more, then, will the blood of Christ, who through the eternal Spirit offered himself unblemished to God, cleanse our consciences from acts that lead to death, so that we may serve the living God" (Hebrews 9:14).

From the time of His baptism by John the Baptist when "the Holy Spirit descended on him" (Luke 3:21), He relied on the Spirit's power to defeat Satan in the wilderness of temptation (Luke 4:1-2) and to go forth in ministry anointed by "the Spirit of the Lord" (Luke 4:18). The apostle Paul makes it clear that it was by the power of the Holy Spirit that Jesus, "through the Spirit of holiness was declared with power to be the Son of God by his resurrection from the dead" (Romans 1:4).

Jesus prepared His disciples for the coming of the Holy Spirit into their lives: "But when he, the Spirit of truth, comes, he will guide you into all truth. He will not speak on his own; he will speak only what he hears, and he will tell you what is yet to come. He will bring glory to me by taking what is mine and making it known to you. All that belongs to the Father is mine. That is why I said the Spirit will take from what is mine and make it known to you" (John 16:13-15).

The Holy Spirit worked mightily through the life and ministry of our Lord Jesus Christ. Jesus insisted that His apostles "stay in the city until . . . clothed with power from on high" (Luke 24:49). The Holy Spirit within them would reveal more about Jesus than they had learned during the three years they were with Him in the flesh. They would then understand more fully what Jesus had taught them than when they had heard it before from His lips. Jesus had promised that the Spirit would "bring glory to me by taking from what is mine and making it known to you" (John 16:14). The disciples were saddened by Jesus' announcement that He was departing. But Jesus sought to encourage them with a prophecy: "your grief will turn to joy" (John 16:20). He knew that the coming of the Holy Spirit upon them would make their "joy complete" (John 16:24).

The coming of the Holy Spirit upon the believers on the day of Pentecost not only assured them that Jesus had been glorified in Heaven but also the outpoured Spirit of Jesus assured them that He was being *coronated* in their hearts. For nearly three years they had been with Him physically; from now on they would be spiritually indwelt by His Spirit. Little wonder that He had explained it would be better for Him to depart in the flesh in order to return in the Spirit: "It is for your good that I am going away. Unless I go away, the Counselor will not come to you; but if I go, I will send him to you" (John 16:7).

Sometimes I hear believers today ask, "Wouldn't it have been a wonderful thing to have lived in Jesus' time on earth and gazed on Him and listened, along with His disciples, to the things He taught and watched Him do the miracles of healing the sick and raising the dead?" I certainly agree that such moments would have been wonderful! But to be honest, I know that my relationship with Jesus Christ today is more glorious because I've been born anew by the Holy Spirit. I've been cleansed and filled with the Holy Spirit. And from time to time I am asking for fresh fillings of the Holy Spirit in order to live in holiness and power and in intimate fellowship with Jesus—all by living in fellowship with an ungrieved Holy Spirit.

But let us consider the work of the Holy Spirit within us as we turn to the finality of our salvation. Paul the apostle sets forth a glorious truth about our eternal future when he declares, "You, however, are not controlled by the sinful nature but by the Spirit, if the Spirit of God lives in you. And if anyone does not have the Spirit of Christ, he does not belong to Christ. But if Christ is in you, your body is dead because of sin, yet your spirit is alive because of righteousness. And if the Spirit of him who raised Jesus from the dead is living in you, he who raised Christ from the dead will also give life to your mortal bodies through his Spirit, who lives in you" (Romans 8:9-11).

Being born of the Spirit means a moral and spiritual resurrection; this new birth leads to life in the power of the Holy Spirit—cleansing from sin; empowerment for worship, prayer, and works of righteousness; and the joy and hope of the eternal life already begun.

We see in Paul's passage of Romans 8:9-11 (above) our hope of a physical resurrection by the power of the same Spirit who brought about our moral and spiritual resurrection in the new birth. Our salvation from first to last—justification, sanctification, and glorification—are all works of the Holy Spirit bringing to pass what Christ's death on the cross provided. We are assured that we who live and walk in the Spirit shall be resurrected in the last days.

But in our daily walk with Christ, we are indebted to the indwelling Holy Spirit for His faithfulness to share with us the life of Christ. The apostle Paul expressed disappointment in the Galatian believers because they did not realize the need to properly relate to the

Holy Spirit for the power to continue in Christ-likeness. He scolded, "Are you so foolish? After beginning with the Spirit, are you now trying to attain your goal by human effort?" (Galatians 3:3).

Jesus is our example for daily living in the power of the Spirit. In His incarnation, Jesus laid aside His divine attributes until there remained nothing to distinguish Him from other men. Being empty, the Father filled Him with the Holy Spirit beyond measure. He let His disciples know that He spoke and worked only as the Spirit constrained Him to speak and work. His entire ministry on earth was spent in living the Spirit-filled, Spirit-led, Spirit-anointed life.

It is interesting that Jesus had little to say about the Holy Spirit early in His ministry. But near the end He explained His and the Father's plan to send the Holy Spirit to them. He held their attention as He began revealing the purpose of the Spirit's coming on them (John, chapters 14-16). He would be their *Paraclete* (One coming alongside them as a Helper). He would comfort, counsel, and convict. Apart from the power of the Holy Spirit, they would not succeed in their commission to take the Gospel to the ends of the earth. And no Christian believer can live the Christian life successfully apart from the power of the Holy Spirit.

Prayer: Father God, thank You for sending Your one and only Son Jesus to planet earth to die an atoning death for our sins. And thank You that Jesus was filled beyond measure with the Holy Spirit to demonstrate for us how life in the Spirit is to be lived. Lord, help us to be grateful to You for all that You gave up in order to be filled with the Spirit without measure—You were full of the Holy Spirit. May we be willing to deny ourselves, surrender our pride, repent of our selfishness, and ask in faith for the fullness of Your Spirit. Help us understand that this is the only way to experience the power for holiness of heart and life. Teach us how to ask for and receive the fullness of Your Holy Spirit and how to glorify You. Amen!

28

"Be Filled with the Spirit"

"And do not be drunk with wine, in which is dissipation; but be filled with the Spirit" (Ephesians 5:18, NKJV).

The Holy Spirit is given to the believer in the experience of the new birth. Actually, the Spirit administers the new birth. Jesus explained to Nicodemus, "What is born of the flesh is flesh, and what is born of the Spirit is spirit" (John 3:6, NRSV). Being "born of the Spirit" brings about the spiritual miracle of eternal life. It is essential that the new Christian soon learn how to relate to the Holy Spirit.

New Testament Scriptures repeatedly speak of the "fullness" of the Spirit. Jesus spoke of the "abundant" life, and He promised that "if you . . . know how to give good gifts to your children, how much more will *your* heavenly Father give the Holy Spirit to those who ask Him!" (Luke 11:13, NKJV).

Since it is possible to "grieve" the Spirit (Ephesians 4:30), "quench" the Spirit (I Thessalonians 5:19), or "disobey" the Spirit, we are commanded to "be filled with the Spirit." Greek scholars caution that this command is given in the present tense and should therefore be translated, *"keep on being filled with the Spirit."* There should be an initial filling of the Holy Spirit in every believer's life when they learn of Jesus' promise of such a milestone in the Christian journey. But we must not forget the imperative here includes subsequent refillings of the Spirit.

When I was once asked by a pastor why we need fresh fillings of the Spirit, I replied, "Because many of us leak a lot—we do at unguarded moments yield to the flesh by attitudes, expressions, and negligence in spiritual disciplines. These shortfalls, while they may not be major sins, do matter to our holy Guest. We soon realize that we have lost ground, and our response should be *asking for the much-moreness of the Holy Spirit*.

Most of my life in ministry has been spent in the pastorate. When I was in seminary, I accepted a student pastorate at the age of nineteen. I spent the next forty-five years pastoring churches. But during the last 21 years, I've traveled the nation preaching on spiritual renewal. I am amazed at the number of evangelical Christians who tell me, "I have never asked God to fill me with the Holy Spirit." But I'm delighted at the response of those—not all, but many—who are hungry for the fullness of the Holy Spirit for the fellowship, inspiration, and power for holy living they hear is available in the Spirit-filled life.

Let us consider some of the steps to the fullness of the Holy Spirit. These are given with the assumption that the reader is a born-again believer and is sincere in following the teachings of our Lord Jesus Christ and His apostles as laid out in the New Testament Scriptures.

• *Humbling*. Both humility and honesty are required before we can be filled with the Spirit. We need humility to admit our need—falling short of Christ's command to love God with all our hearts and to love our brothers and sisters even as we love ourselves, and not being faithful in prayer. These are only some of the things that reveal weaknesses in our spiritual lives and our need of the power of the Holy Spirit. We need humility to *confess* these sins to God and to *acknowledge* them to others; and then we need to *repent,* meaning that with His forgiveness and strength we will turn from our weakness to His strength in the Spirit.

• *Hungering*. Jesus said, "Blessed are those who hunger and thirst for righteousness, for they will be filled" (Matthew 5:6, (NRSV). Casual interest and curiosity aren't sufficient for receiving the fullness of the Holy Spirit; there must be genuine hunger, the kind for which one is willing to sacrifice. But, I don't mean that we bargain for the Holy Spirit. The Holy Spirit is promised by the Father and the Son, but He is not a Gift thrown at just any bargain hunter.

- *Surrendering.* As Christian believers, we have been bought at a great price; "You know that you were ransomed from the futile ways inherited from your ancestors, not with perishable things like silver or gold, but with the precious blood of Christ, like that of a lamb without defect or blemish" (I Peter 1:18-19, NRSV). Christ has a redeemed claim on His born-again believer, but He appeals to us for total surrender: "I appeal to you therefore, brothers and sisters, by the mercies of God, to present your bodies as a living sacrifice, holy and acceptable to God, which is your spiritual worship. Do not be conformed to this world, but be transformed by the renewing of your minds, so that you may discern what is the will of God—what is good and acceptable and perfect" (Romans 12:1-2, NRSV).

- *Asking, Seeking, Knocking.* In chapter 11 of Luke, we find the disciples impressed with the praying of Jesus. They request, "Lord, teach us to pray" (Luke 11:1). Our Lord not only sets forth a model prayer, but He extends His teachings to include the kind of gifts the Father gives to those who seek His will. In fact, He makes it clear that the Father gives good gifts, particularly when it comes to the Gift of the Holy Spirit. He has already given the Gift of the Holy Spirit to the believer in the new birth, even though the believer did not ask for Him. But when it comes to the fullness of the Holy Spirit, the believer must ask. John Knox reminded the Christians of His day that this best Gift is not given without our asking. In asking for the Holy Spirit, Jesus emphasizes persistence when he says to *ask, seek, and knock,* representing a graduating intensity in the urgent search for the fullness of the Holy Spirit: (1) *Ask,* meaning state your need, file your claim; (2) *Seek,* meaning an all-out search; and (3) *Knock,* meaning a will-have-at-any-cost determination. Actually, within the context of seeking for the abundance of the Holy Spirit, Jesus promises, "If you then, who are evil, know how to give good gifts to your children, how much more will the heavenly Father give the Holy Spirit to those who ask him" (Luke 11:13, NRSV).

• *Believing.* Just as we were saved by faith, we are sanctified and filled with the Holy Spirit by faith. When a totally humble, hungry, surrendered, seeking heart asks the Father for the fullness of the Holy Spirit, there is no place for doubt. Our prayer should be the test of our faith; the proof of the answer is God's power in our lives after the prayer—a loving heart to forgive, an anointing for prayer, strength for resisting temptation, a holy boldness for witness, and a joyous resolve to endure the opposition of the world, the flesh, and the devil. When we ask our heavenly Father for the fullness of the Holy Spirit, let us never offend Him by doubting that He answered.

• *Obeying.* We get up from the prayer and go out to obey the Word of God in our Christian living. That's what the apostles did after they were filled with the Holy Spirit on the day of Pentecost. They soon ran into the opposition of the religious authorities and were ordered to no longer teach and preach in the name of Jesus. The apostles answered, "We must obey God rather than any human authority . . . we are witnesses to these things, and so is the Holy Spirit whom God has given to those who obey him" (Acts 5:29 and 32, NRSV). It is by experience as obedient children of God that our communion in prayer and our sensitivity to the Holy Spirit often brings a greater measure of the Spirit's power.

• *Renewing.* Let us keep on seeking the power of the Holy Spirit. Our heavenly Father never meant to grant us in one fell swoop an experience with the Holy Spirit to last a lifetime. He wants to keep on filling and refilling us with His Spirit as we obey Him. He has much for each one of us to do, but everything we do should be done in the power of the Holy Spirit if it is to count for eternity.

It is my considered opinion that in these times the greatest need of the Church of Jesus Christ is for believers to get serious about the Spirit-filled life and commit to a search for His fullness.

Prayer: Lord, since You have promised that if I would ask for the Holy Spirit, my heavenly Father would give me the Holy Spirit. I long for the fullness of the Holy Spirit, and I'm now asking for this promised fullness. I'm told in Your Word that if I asked I would receive; if I sought, I would find; and if I knocked, the door would be opened to His fullness.

Taking You at Your Word, I'm now believing that it is true that in my life I am full of the Holy Spirit. I'm trusting Your Word which declares that You give the Holy Spirit to those who obey You (Acts 5:32).

Thank You for filling me with the Holy Spirit! Amen!

29

The Fullness of the Holy Spirit

"Nevertheless, when the Son of Man comes, will He find faith on the earth?" (Luke 18:8, RSV).

At this late hour of the Church age the case must be made for the Spirit-filled life. Never in centuries of Christianity has evil been more determined to defeat righteousness. Satan is in these times releasing from the classrooms and training grounds his most brilliant, bold, and brutal principalities and powers of darkness against the Church and the world.

Christians must awaken to the realization that we have fallen short of the standard for spiritual power that Jesus and His apostles set for His Church. We must believe that our Sovereign Christ, to whom all power in Heaven and on earth and under the earth has been given, is seeking to rally the saints to prevail with Him for what might be the final great awakening before the Second Coming. Despite false prophets, apostasy, cold hearts, lost battles, and a great falling away, we must still believe that God is seeking an anointed army of spiritual warriors here on earth to align itself with His Heavenly hosts for a mighty tidal wave of the outpoured Spirit.

It appears to this writer that our Sovereign Christ would love to close out the Church age with the greatest revival in all of Church history. It is high time for Christian believers in all parts of the world to get serious about the Spirit-filled life. This would mean sincere heart-searching, repentance, and a return to sacrificial praying of the Scriptures. This would also mean a return to the kind of faith Jesus hoped to find in the end times.

What would be a few of the elements of such an experience? These are elements of the Spirit-filled life that would be found in any culture:

• *Fire.* Jesus said, "I have come to bring fire on the earth, and how I wish it were already kindled" (Luke 12:49). I believe that Jesus had in mind the same kind of fire that John the Baptist was referring to when he prophesied what Jesus would do in the nature of His baptizing: "I baptize you with water for repentance. But after me will come one who is more powerful than I, whose sandals I am not fit to carry. He will baptize you with the Holy Spirit and with fire. His winnowing fork is in his hand, and he will clear his threshing floor, gathering his wheat into the barn and burning up the chaff with unquenchable fire" (Matthew 3:11-12).

Fire is a symbol for both cleansing and judgment. The death and resurrection of Jesus Christ served a judgment on an apostate religion and a sinful society. He set the world aflame with a new beginning of hope that burned its way into believing hearts. On His resurrection morning, Jesus came upon two of His disciples on the Emmaus Road. They were downcast, confused, and fear-stricken. After a time with Jesus, they were transformed. When Jesus had gone, the two looked at each other and exclaimed, "Were not our hearts burning within us while he talked with us on the road and opened the Scriptures to us" (Luke 24:32).

And then there were the fires of Pentecost. "When the day of Pentecost came, they were all together in one place. Suddenly a sound like the blowing of a violent wind came from heaven and filled the whole house where they were sitting. They saw what seemed to be tongues of fire that separated and came to rest on each of them" (Acts 2:1-3). It seems that the fire came in one great cluster, then divided so that a tongue of fire sat above the head of each of the 120 believers. Perhaps we are to understand this to emphasize the unity of the Spirit within the diversity of the represented believers. Most evangelical scholars believe the fire signifies the purification and cleansing of the hearts of each one. I feel quite certain that the phenomenon of fire was a fulfillment of John the Baptist's prophecy that Jesus would baptize His followers "with the Holy Spirit and with fire" (Matthew 3:11; Luke 3:16).

The apostle Paul once advised his spiritual son Timothy to "rekindle the gift of God that is within you through the laying on of my hands" (II Timothy 1:6, NRSV). The reference here is to the anointing of the Holy Spirit which had come much earlier in Timothy's life as Paul had ministered to him. The Spirit was still with Timothy, but Paul sensed that it was time for a renewing, a refilling, and a fresh quickening of the Spirit—a rekindling of the Spirit's fire. Then the apostle assured his younger colleague, "God did not give us a spirit of cowardice, but rather a spirit of power and of love and of self-discipline" (II Timothy 1:7, NRSV).

• *Faith.* The first Christian martyr was Stephen, and he is described as "a man full of faith and of the Holy Spirit" (Acts 6:5). The same characterization is given of Barnabas. Neither of these Spirit-filled men were apostles in the official sense, but they were full of the Holy Spirit and were mighty men of faith. The Holy Spirit is the Spirit of faith. He imparts *saving* faith to the penitent sinner. He imparts *sanctifying* faith to the thirsty believer seeking the fullness of the Spirit. He imparts *serving* faith to the obedient servant.

Spirit-filled servants advance the kingdom of God through prayer. Jesus gave a parable about a persistent widow of faith who prevailed on an unjust judge to hear her case. The judge cared nothing about her cause, and he only heard her case to escape her persistence. Jesus contrasted our Heavenly Father with the unjust judge by saying, "And will not God bring about justice for his chosen ones, who cry out to him day and night? Will he keep putting them off? I tell you, he will see that they get justice, and quickly" (Luke 18:6-8). And then listen to the concern Jesus had for prayer warriors of persistent faith as He closes the parable: "However, when the Son of Man comes, will he find faith on the earth?" (Luke 18:8). Without a doubt, Jesus is referring to the kind of faith demonstrated by the persistent widow. To continue interceding for a Kingdom cause requires the renewing of our faith by the Holy Spirit within us. When we know we are praying in accordance with the will of God, we must ask the Holy Spirit to increase and embolden our faith.

• *Freedom.* There is a sense in which the truth, as it is in Jesus, sets us free. As He promised His followers, "you will know the truth, and the truth will set you free" (John 8:32). And, "if the Son sets you free, you will be free indeed" (John 8:36). The apostle Paul reminded the Galatian believers that they had been liberated from the bondage of the law: "It is for freedom that Christ has set us free. Stand firm, then, and do not let yourselves be burdened again by a yoke of slavery" (Galatians 5:1). It is sad to see Christians become enslaved by legalism and religious dogma. Such a condition will often produce "the works of the flesh" rather than "the fruit of the Spirit."

We also see in the book of Galatians that *love is the essence of our spiritual freedom in Christ*: "For in Christ Jesus neither circumcision nor uncircumcision has any value. The only thing that counts is faith expressing itself through love" (Galatians 5:6).

To the Galatian church Paul made it clear that only life in the Spirit empowers the believer for victory over the flesh: "So I say, live by the Spirit, and you will not gratify the desires of the sinful nature. For the sinful nature desires what is contrary to the Spirit, and the Spirit what is contrary to the sinful nature. They are in conflict with each other, so that you do not do what you want. But if you are led by the Spirit, you are not under law" (Galatians 5:16-18).

The apostle Paul emphasizes the freedom of the Spirit in the experience of sanctification. Writing to the Corinthians, he explains: "Now the Lord is the Spirit, and where the Spirit of the Lord is, there is freedom. And we, who with unveiled faces all reflect the Lord's glory, are being transformed into his likeness with ever-increasing glory, which comes from the Lord, who is the Spirit" (II Corinthians 3:17-18).

The Holy Spirit is a Gift of God to the believing heart in the moment of the new birth. That same Spirit will convince the born-again believer of the need for cleansing from sin. The obedient believer will repent of sin, surrender completely to Christ, ask for the sanctifying experience, and by faith experience a purified heart. This is *crisis sanctification*. But in the II Corinthian passage above, we hear the apostle Paul describing *progressive sanctification*. The Holy Spirit is absolutely and eternally holy, and it is His redemptive work to not only convict the unbelievers and bring them into the new birth experience, but it is His work also to cleanse believers from sin and enable them to take on the likeness of our Lord. Christ is Himself the glory of the Father, and it is the role of the Holy Spirit to transform us gradually to reflect an ever-increasing glory of our Savior. What freedom we have, continually growing all through life into Christ-likeness!

• *Fruit.* "The fullness of the Spirit" is an inspiring expression. Even more so, it is a glorious experience. The new convert can bear a measure of the fruit of the Spirit because the Spirit *indwells* him. The sanctified Christian can bear all the fruit of the Spirit because he is *filled* with the Spirit.

The apostle Paul lists the fruit of the Spirit in Galatians 5:23: "But the fruit of the Spirit is love, joy, peace, patience, kindness, goodness, faithfulness, gentleness and self-control." Our New Testament does not leave us in the dark as to what the Spirit-filled life is like. It is a life of holiness, a life of Christ-likeness. Commenting on this great holiness passage, Dr. W. T. Purkiser pointed out:

> It sounds as if the apostle should have written, "The *fruits* of the Spirit *are* love, joy, peace . . ." But the grammar is no accident. It can be understood in two different ways. First, the fruit of the Spirit is an indivisible cluster of graces that are never separated. There is one undivided cluster which taken altogether constitutes the fruit of the Spirit. But there is another explanation for the grammar of these verses. It is that Paul means here that the fruit of the Spirit is love, period! What follows are the dimensions of love. (W. T. Purkiser, *God's Spirit in Today's World,* Kansas City, MO: Beacon Hill Press of Kansas City, 1974, pp. 71-72).

• *Love.* The Word of God measures Christian spirituality in terms of love. Love is the first and final test. Jesus, when asked to name the supreme commandment, answered: ". . . you shall love the Lord your God with all your heart, with all your soul, and with all your mind. This is the first and great commandment. And the second is like it: You shall love your neighbor as yourself" (Matthew 22:37-39, NKJV). Again, He said, "A new commandment I give to you, that you love one another; as I have loved you, that you also love one another. By this all will know that you are My disciples, if you have love for one another" (John 13:34-35, NKJV).

If holiness and love are what the Spirit-filled life is about, how does it express itself? Again, Dr. W.T. Purkiser sets forth the Christian life of holiness in eight striking definitions. The defining statements are his, and the elaborations are mine:

JOY

• *Joy is love singing.* Paul tells us, "God has poured out his love into our hearts by the Holy Spirit, whom he has given us" (Romans 5:5). His sanctifying love washes out bitterness, and we are enabled to understand, forgive, and have compassion. The first sign that a Christian is filled with the Holy Spirit is not some phenomenal manifestation, but an inward purifying and healing of our redeemed heart in order that we might love God and others with unconditional love. Such a life not only sings; that life is a joyful song.

PEACE

• *Peace is love resting.* Jesus invited, "Come to me, all you who are weary and burdened, and I will give you rest" (Matthew 11:28). The author of the Hebrew epistle pointed out, "There remains therefore a rest for the people of God" (Hebrews 4:9, NKJV).

Believers are called into a spiritual rest through Jesus Christ. We are no longer to worry about our salvation, nor are we to worry about the necessities of life—food, shelter, clothing, health, etc. When God fills our hearts with His Spirit, we are enabled to rest in His promises and provisions for managing life. Christians who are worried and frantic about the affairs of life are a poor testimony to their loved ones and friends.

PATIENCE

• *Patience is love enduring.* The apostle Paul claimed that love "endures all things" (I Corinthians 13:7, NRSV). The fullness of the Spirit brings the quality of durability. Suffering is allowed to season the life, not sour it. Giving up is not an option for consideration. Perseverance is the mind-set. We know that we are to stay the course no matter what comes. To assure those who endure, the apostle Peter wrote of the joy that awaits them both in this life and in the life to come: "His divine power has given us everything we need for life and godliness through our knowledge of him who called us by his own glory and goodness. Through these he has given us his very great and precious promises, so that through them you may participate in the divine nature and escape the corruption in the world caused by evil desires. For this very reason, make every effort to add to your faith goodness; and to goodness, knowledge; and to knowledge, self-control; and to self-control, perseverance; and to perseverance, godliness; and to godliness, brotherly kindness; and to brotherly kindness, love. For if you possess these qualities in increasing measure, they will keep you from being ineffective and unproductive in your knowledge of our Lord Jesus Christ. But if anyone does not have them, he is nearsighted and blind, and has forgotten that he has been cleansed from his past sins. Therefore, my brothers, be all the more eager to make your calling and election sure. For if you do these things, you will never fall, and you will receive a rich welcome into the eternal kingdom of our Lord and Savior Jesus Christ" (II Peter 1:3-11).

KINDNESS

- *Kindness is love sharing.* Paul said in his Hymn of Love, "Love is kind" (I Corinthians 13:4). Love has to express itself, and when it speaks, it speaks with kindness. It does not wound, bruise, or destroy. A loving heart cannot do such a thing. It speaks the truth in love. The sanctified heart complies with the apostle's order to show love: "Do not let any unwholesome talk come out of your mouths, but only what is helpful for building others up according to their needs, that it may benefit those who listen. And do not grieve the Holy Spirit of God, with whom you were sealed for the day of redemption. Get rid of all bitterness, rage and anger, brawling and slander, along with every form of malice. Be kind and compassionate to one another, forgiving each other, just as in Christ God forgave you" (Ephesians 4:29-32).

GOODNESS

- *Goodness is love's character.* As God's love flows into us and through us, we become more like Him. Paul wrote, "Be imitators of God, therefore, as dearly loved children and live a life of love, just as Christ loved us and gave himself up for us as a fragrant offering and sacrifice to God" (Ephesians 5:1-2). Jesus' self-denial is not only our means of salvation; it is also our example for daily living. Such goodness cannot be missed by either the Church or the world. Nor can we take credit for such a quality of life. Goodness is Christ living out His life through us in the power of the Holy Spirit.

FAITHFULNESS

- *Faithfulness is love's habit.* As Christ was faithful to the Father, so we are called to be faithful to Christ. He is our Master and He expects and commands the kind of stewardship we will not be ashamed of at the Judgment Seat of Christ. Paul wrote, "Now it is required that those who have been given a trust must prove faithful" (I Corinthians 4:2). We should all pray daily that we might run the Christian race with the reward in mind of hearing our Lord say to us in that day, "Well done, good and faithful servant!" In order for this to come true, I dare say there are some things in this life that will not get the attention we were tempted to give them. Let us pray to become more sensitive to the Spirit's eternal value system.

GENTLENESS

- *Gentleness is love's touch.* I think the Bible has more to say about a nonviolent nature than most of us realize. Paul wrote, "I urge you to live a life worthy of the calling you have received. Be completely humble and gentle; be patient, bearing with one another in love. Make every effort to keep the unity of the Spirit through the bond of peace" (Ephesians 4:1-3). The same apostle told Timothy how leaders were to set an example of love's touch: ". . . be temperate, self-controlled, respectable, hospitable . . . not given to drunkenness, not violent but gentle, not quarrelsome" (I Timothy 3:2-3 NIV). The more we yield to the Holy Spirit, the more He will impart to us the gentle nature of our loving Lord.

SELF-CONTROL

- *Self-control is love in charge.* This aspect of the fruit of the Spirit is sometimes translated "temperance." But it is far more than that. It has to do with the mastery of self in all areas of desire and impulse. The Spirit-empowered Christian overcomes "the works of the flesh." Paul the apostle puts it to us in a direct manner: "So I say, live by the Spirit, and you will not gratify the desires of the sinful nature. For the sinful nature desires what is contrary to the Spirit, and the Spirit what is contrary to the sinful nature. They are in conflict with each other, so that you do not do what you want" (Galatians 5:16-17). A characteristic of the sanctified life is that our thoughts, desires, temperaments, conversations, and habits are under control, and we are living a life that is pleasing our Lord Jesus Christ. The crying need of our times is for Christians to *seek* and *find* and *live* in the fullness of the Spirit.

Despite the wickedness of the world and the weakness of the Church, it is my prayerfully considered opinion that an epidemic of prevailing prayer must break forth soon if our merciful God is to see that His people are meeting the conditions of His promise: "If my people, who are called by my name, will humble themselves and pray and seek my face and turn from their wicked ways, then will I hear from heaven and will forgive their sins and will heal their land" (II Chronicles 7:14). Only Spirit-anointed prayer will move God to pour out His Spirit on His universal Church to produce the results He requires of the Church and the world.

Prayer: Lord, we need to bear fruit—more fruit and much fruit. You are faithful to tell us, "By this My Father is glorified" and we prove to be Your disciples (John 15:8, NKJV). Forgive our fruitlessness and our failure to abide in You consistently and increasingly. We worship You, Lord Jesus, as the "true vine" and the Father as the "vinedresser" (John 15:1). Forbid, Lord, that we should be cast out as a branch and wither! Rather, rekindle the fires of the Spirit within us and help us maintain the fire and glory to bear the fruit! Amen!

ABOUT THE AUTHOR

James W. Tharp was ordained in the Church of the Nazarene in 1957. He has pastored churches in Indiana, Pennsylvania, California, New Mexico, Washington, and Montana. His ministry is dedicated to preparing the Church through prayer for another great spiritual awakening.

In 1979, he began working with the Billy Graham Evangelistic Association, assisting the evangelist in his telephone counseling ministry. He was the personal guest of Billy Graham for the 10 days of "Amsterdam '86".

From 1979-1981, Tharp lectured on the Holy Spirit for California Graduate School of Theology in their doctorate program. He pursued further studies at Olivet Nazarene University in Kankakee, Illinois, and at Seattle Pacific University. Since 1994 he has been devoted to speaking in camp meetings, revivals, and pastoral institutes and conducting the School of Prayer, helping thousands to improve their prayer lives and deepen their Christian walk.

Tharp is the founder and president of CHRISTIAN RENEWAL MINISTRIES based in Bozeman, Montana (formerly in Dothan, Alabama). He is the editor of a quarterly publication, *Christian Renewal Journal*. His blog is revivalpray.blogspot.com.

MORE BOOKS by James W. Tharp

ESTELLE

REVIVAL MUST COME!

THE SPIRIT OF PRAYER

Available from amazon.com
Also available from crmin.org

AUDIO MESSAGES by James W. Tharp

SCHOOL OF PRAYER
(Album of 8 CDs and Notebook)

REVIVAL & CAMP MEETING MESSAGES
(6 CDs, 12 Messages)

Available from crmin.org

www.ingramcontent.com/pod-product-compliance
Lightning Source LLC
Chambersburg PA
CBHW061948070426
42450CB00007BA/1089